Wonderful ways to prepare

BARBECUES

by ANNETTE HALCOMB

OTHER TITLES IN THIS SERIES

Wonderful ways to prepare

BARBECUES

PLAYMORE INC NEW YORK USA
UNDER ARRANGEMENT WITH
I. WALDMAN & SON INC

AYERS & JAMES PTY LTD
CROWS NEST AUSTRALIA

STAFFORD PEMBERTON PUBLISHING
KNUTSFORD UNITED KINGDOM

FIRST PUBLISHED 1978

PUBLISHED IN THE USA
BY PLAYMORE INC.
UNDER ARRANGEMENT WITH I. WALDMAN & SON INC.

PUBLISHED IN AUSTRALIA
BY AYERS & JAMES PTY. LTD.
CROWS NEST.   AUSTRALIA

PUBLISHED IN THE UNITED KINGDOM
BY STAFFORD PEMBERTON PUBLISHING
KNUTSFORD CHESIRE

COPYRIGHT © 1978
AYERS & JAMES PTY. LTD.
5 ALEXANDER STREET
CROWS NEST   N.S.W.   AUSTRALIA

THIS BOOK MAY NOT BE REPRODUCED IN PART
OR FULL, BY ANY MEANS, NOR TRANSLATED, NOR
TRANSMITTED WITHOUT THE WRITTEN PERMISSION
OF THE PUBLISHER

ISBN 0 86908 062 8

OVEN TEMPERATURE GUIDE

Description	Gas		Electric		Mark
	C	F	C	F	
Cool	100	200	110	225	¼
Very Slow	120	250	120	250	½
Slow	150	300	150	300	1-2
Moderately slow	160	325	170	340	3
Moderate	180	350	200	400	4
Moderately hot	190	375	220	425	5-6
Hot	200	400	230	450	6-7
Very hot	230	450	250	475	8-9

LIQUID MEASURES

IMPERIAL	METRIC
1 teaspoon	5 ml
1 tablespoon	20 ml
2 fluid ounces (¼ cup)	62.5 ml
4 fluid ounces (½ cup)	125 ml
8 fluid ounces (1 cup)	250 ml
1 pint (16 ounces — 2 cups)*	500 ml

* (The imperial pint is equal to 20 fluid ounces.)

SOLID MEASURES

AVOIRDUPOIS	METRIC
1 ounce	30 g
4 ounces (¼ lb)	125 g
8 ounces (½ lb)	250 g
12 ounces (¾ lb)	375 g
16 ounces (1 lb)	500 g
24 ounces (1½ lb)	750 g
32 ounces (2 lb)	1000 g (1 kg)

CUP AND SPOON REPLACEMENTS FOR OUNCES

INGREDIENT	½ oz	1 oz	2 oz	3 oz	4 oz	5 oz	6 oz	7 oz	8 oz
Almonds, ground	2 T	¼ C	½ C	¾ C	1¼ C	1⅓ C	1⅔ C	2 C	2¼ C
slivered	6 t	¼ C	½ C	¾ C	1 C	1⅓ C	1⅔ C	2 C	2¼ C
whole	2 T	¼ C	⅓ C	½ C	¾ C	1 C	1¼ C	1⅓ C	1½ C
Apples, dried whole	3 T	½ C	1 C	1⅓ C	2 C	2⅓ C	2¾ C	3⅓ C	3¾ C
Apricots, chopped	2 T	¼ C	½ C	¾ C	1 C	1¼ C	1½ C	1¾ C	2 C
whole	2 T	3 T	½ C	⅔ C	1 C	1¼ C	1⅓ C	1½ C	1¾ C
Arrowroot	1 T	2 T	⅓ C	½ C	⅔ C	¾ C	1 C	1¼ C	1⅓ C
Baking Powder	1 T	2 T	⅓ C	½ C	⅔ C	¾ C	1 C	1 C	1¼ C
Baking Soda	1 T	2 T	⅓ C	½ C	⅔ C	¾ C	1 C	1 C	1¼ C
Barley	1 T	2 T	¼ C	½ C	⅔ C	¾ C	1 C	1 C	1¼ C
Breadcrumbs, dry	2 T	¼ C	½ C	¾ C	1 C	1¼ C	1½ C	1¾ C	2 C
soft	¼ C	½ C	1 C	1½ C	2 C	2½ C	3 C	3⅔ C	4¼ C
Biscuit Crumbs	2 T	¼ C	½ C	¾ C	1¼ C	1⅓ C	1⅔ C	2 C	2¼ C
Butter	3 t	6 t	¼ C	⅓ C	½ C	⅔ C	¾ C	1 C	1 C
Cheese, grated, lightly packed,									
natural cheddar	6 t	¼ C	½ C	¾ C	1 C	1¼ C	1½ C	1¾ C	2 C
Processed cheddar	5 t	2 T	⅓ C	⅔ C	¾ C	1 C	1¼ C	1½ C	1⅔ C
Parmesan, Romano	6 t	¼ C	½ C	¾ C	1 C	1⅓ C	1⅔ C	2 C	2¼ C
Cherries, candied, chopped	1 T	2 T	⅓ C	½ C	¾ C	1 C	1 C	1⅓ C	1½ C
whole	1 T	2 T	⅓ C	½ C	⅔ C	¾ C	1 C	1¼ C	1⅓ C
Cocoa	2 T	¼ C	½ C	¾ C	1¼ C	1⅓ C	1⅔ C	2 C	2¼ C
Coconut, desiccated	2 T	⅓ C	⅔ C	1 C	1⅓ C	1⅔ C	2 C	2⅓ C	2⅔ C
shredded	⅓ C	⅔ C	1¼ C	1¾ C	2½ C	3 C	3⅔ C	4⅓ C	5 C
Cornstarch	6 t	3 T	½ C	⅔ C	1 C	1¼ C	1½ C	1⅔ C	2 C
Corn Syrup	2 t	1 T	2 T	¼ C	⅓ C	½ C	½ C	⅔ C	⅔ C
Coffee, ground	2 T	⅓ C	⅔ C	1 C	1⅓ C	1⅔ C	2 C	2⅓ C	2⅔ C
instant	3 T	½ C	1 C	1⅓ C	1¾ C	2¼ C	2⅔ C	3 C	3½ C
Cornflakes	½ C	1 C	2 C	3 C	4¼ C	5¼ C	6¼ C	7⅓C	8⅓ C
Cream of Tartar	1 T	2 T	⅓ C	½ C	⅔ C	¾ C	1 C	1 C	1¼ C
Currants	1 T	2 T	⅓ C	⅔ C	¾ C	1 C	1¼ C	1½ C	1⅔ C
Custard Powder	6 t	3 T	½ C	⅔ C	1 C	1¼ C	1½ C	1⅔ C	2 C
Dates, chopped	1 T	2 T	⅓ C	⅔ C	¾ C	1 C	1¼ C	1½ C	1⅔ C
whole, pitted	1 T	2 T	⅓ C	½ C	¾ C	1 C	1¼ C	1⅓ C	1½ C
Figs, chopped	1 T	2 T	⅓ C	½ C	¾ C	1 C	1 C	1⅓ C	1½ C
Flour, all-purpose or cake	6 t	¼ C	½ C	¾ C	1 C	1¼ C	1½ C	1¾ C	2 C
wholemeal	6 t	3 T	½ C	⅔ C	1 C	1¼ C	1⅓ C	1⅔ C	1¾ C
Fruit, mixed	1 T	2 T	⅓ C	½ C	¾ C	1 C	1¼ C	1⅓ C	1½ C
Gelatine	5 t	2 T	⅓ C	½ C	¾ C	1 C	1 C	1¼ C	1½ C
Ginger, crystallised pieces	1 T	2 T	⅓ C	½ C	¾ C	1 C	1¼ C	1⅓ C	1½ C
ground	6 t	⅓ C	½ C	¾ C	1¼ C	1½ C	1¾ C	2 C	2¼ C
preserved, heavy syrup	1 T	2 T	⅓ C	½ C	⅔ C	¾ C	1 C	1 C	1¼ C
Glucose, liquid	2 t	1 T	2 T	¼ C	⅓ C	½ C	½ C	⅔ C	⅔ C
Haricot Beans	1 T	2 T	⅓ C	½ C	⅔ C	¾ C	1 C	1 C	1¼ C

In this table, t represents teaspoonful, T represents tablespoonful and C represents cupful.

CUP AND SPOON REPLACEMENTS FOR OUNCES (Cont.)

INGREDIENT	½ oz	1 oz	2 oz	3 oz	4 oz	5 oz	6 oz	7 oz	8 oz
Honey	2 t	1 T	2 T	¼ C	⅓ C	½ C	½ C	⅔ C	⅔ C
Jam	2 t	1 T	2 T	¼ C	⅓ C	½ C	½ C	⅔ C	¾ C
Lentils	1 T	2 T	⅓ C	½ C	⅔ C	¾ C	1 C	1 C	1¼ C
Macaroni (see pasta)									
Milk Powder, full cream	2 T	¼ C	½ C	¾ C	1¼ C	1⅓ C	1⅔ C	2 C	2¼ C
non fat	2 T	⅓ C	¾ C	1¼ C	1½ C	2 C	2⅓ C	2¾ C	3¼ C
Nutmeg	6 t	3 T	½ C	⅔ C	¾ C	1 C	1¼ C	1½ C	1⅔ C
Nuts, chopped	6 t	¼ C	½ C	¾ C	1 C	1¼ C	1½ C	1¾ C	2 C
Oatmeal	1 T	2 T	½ C	⅔ C	¾ C	1 C	1¼ C	1½ C	1⅔ C
Olives, whole	1 T	2 T	⅓ C	⅔ C	¾ C	1 C	1¼ C	1½ C	1⅔ C
sliced	1 T	2 T	⅓ C	⅔ C	¾ C	1 C	1¼ C	1½ C	1⅔ C
Pasta, short (e.g. macaroni)	1 T	2 T	⅓ C	⅔ C	¾ C	1 C	1¼ C	1½ C	1⅔ C
Peaches, dried & whole	1 T	2 T	⅓ C	⅔ C	¾ C	1 C	1¼ C	1½ C	1⅔ C
chopped	6 t	¼ C	½ C	¾ C	1 C	1¼ C	1½ C	1¾ C	2 C
Peanuts, shelled, raw, whole	1 T	2 T	⅓ C	½ C	¾ C	1 C	1¼ C	1⅓ C	1½ C
roasted	1 T	2 T	⅓ C	⅔ C	¾ C	1 C	1¼ C	1½ C	1⅔ C
Peanut Butter	3 t	6 t	3 T	⅓ C	½ C	½ C	⅔ C	¾ C	1 C
Peas, split	1 T	2 T	⅓ C	½ C	⅔ C	¾ C	1 C	1 C	1¼ C
Peel, mixed	1 T	2 T	⅓ C	½ C	¾ C	1 C	1 C	1¼ C	1½ C
Potato, powder	1 T	2 T	¼ C	⅓ C	½ C	⅔ C	¾ C	1 C	1¼ C
flakes	¼ C	½ C	1 C	1⅓ C	2 C	2⅓ C	2¾ C	3⅓ C	3¾ C
Prunes, chopped	1 T	2 T	⅓ C	½ C	⅔ C	¾ C	1 C	1¼ C	1⅓ C
whole pitted	1 T	2 T	⅓ C	½ C	⅔ C	¾ C	1 C	1 C	1¼ C
Raisins	2 T	¼ C	⅓ C	½ C	¾ C	1 C	1 C	1⅓ C	1½ C
Rice, short grain, raw	1 T	2 T	¼ C	½ C	⅔ C	¾ C	1 C	1 C	1¼ C
long grain, raw	1 T	2 T	⅓ C	½ C	¾ C	1 C	1¼ C	1⅓ C	1½ C
Rice Bubbles	⅔ C	1¼ C	2½ C	3⅔ C	5 C	6¼ C	7½ C	8¾ C	10 C
Rolled Oats	2 T	⅓ C	⅔ C	1 C	1⅓ C	1¾ C	2 C	2½ C	2¾ C
Sago	2 T	¼ C	⅓ C	½ C	¾ C	1 C	1 C	1¼ C	1½ C
Salt, common	3 t	6 t	¼ C	⅓ C	½ C	⅔ C	¾ C	1 C	1 C
Semolina	1 T	2 T	⅓ C	½ C	¾ C	1 C	1 C	1⅓ C	1½ C
Spices	6 t	3 T	¼ C	⅓ C	½ C	½ C	⅔ C	¾ C	1 C
Sugar, plain	3 t	6 t	¼ C	⅓ C	½ C	⅔ C	¾ C	1 C	1 C
confectioners'	1 T	2 T	⅓ C	½ C	¾ C	1 C	1 C	1¼ C	1½ C
moist brown	1 T	2 T	⅓ C	½ C	¾ C	1 C	1 C	1⅓ C	1½ C
Tapioca	1 T	2 T	⅓ C	½ C	⅔ C	¾ C	1 C	1¼ C	1⅓ C
Treacle	2 t	1 T	2 T	¼ C	⅓ C	½ C	½ C	⅔ C	⅔ C
Walnuts, chopped	2 T	¼ C	½ C	¾ C	1 C	1¼ C	1½ C	1¾ C	2 C
halved	2 T	⅓ C	⅔ C	1 C	1¼ C	1½ C	1¾ C	2¼ C	2½ C
Yeast, dried	6 t	3 T	½ C	⅔ C	1 C	1¼ C	1⅓ C	1⅔ C	1¾ C
compressed	3 t	6 t	3 T	⅓ C	½ C	½ C	⅔ C	¾ C	1 C

In this table, t represents teaspoonful, T represents tablespoonful and C represents cupful.

Contents

Sauces, Marinades and Dressings

Plum Sauce

1 425 g can purple plums
2 small onions, finely chopped
2 cloves garlic, crushed
1 tablespoon oil
½ teaspoon ground allspice
½ teaspoon ground ginger

pinch ground cloves
pinch hot chilli pepper
¼ teaspoon salt
2 tablespoons malt or cider
vinegar

1. Remove stones from plums and press plums and liquid through a sieve or whirl in a blender.
2. Saute onion and garlic in oil.
3. Add puréed plums and remaining ingredients.
4. Cover and simmer for 20 minutes.
5. Thicken with a little cornstarch if desired, but not if it is to be stored before use.

Makes 1½ cups (375 ml) sauce.

This sauce may be used with barbecued pork and all cuts beef.

Peanut Butter Sauce

½ cup chopped onions
2 cloves crushed garlic
2 tablespoons oil
½ cup (125 ml) water
1 tablespoon chilli powder

1 tablespoon sugar
4 tablespoons peanut butter
2 tablespoons soya sauce
2 tablespoons lemon juice
1 teaspoon salt

1. Cook onions and garlic in oil.
2. Add water, chilli powder, sugar and peanut butter.
3. Cook until it thickens, stirring gently all the time.
4. Add soya sauce, lemon juice and salt and stir well.

Hot Dog Sauce

1 large onion, chopped
3 tablespoons vegetable oil
2 tablespoons cornstarch
1 dessertspoon curry powder

¼ teaspoon allspice
1 teaspoon salt
1 can (500 g) crushed pineapple
2 tablespoons cider or wine vinegar

1. Saute onion in oil in a large pan until soft.
2. Mix cornstarch, curry powder, allspice and salt in a cup. Stir into onion mixture. Cook stirring constantly until bubbly.
3. Stir in crushed pineapple and vinegar.
4. Cook over low heat stirring constantly until mixture thickens and boils, simmer for 15 minutes.

Serve with frankfurters as a sauce or dip.

Hot Barbecue Sauce

2 teaspoons Tabasco sauce
2½ cups tomato purée
1 teaspoon chilli peppers, minced
¾ cup (187½ ml) oil
½ cup (125 ml) lemon juice

2 tablespoons vinegar
2 cups chopped onion
2 minced cloves garlic
1 tablespoon dry mustard
1 teaspoon salt

1. Mix all ingredients with ½ cup (125 ml) water.
2. Bring to boil.
3. Reduce and simmer for 29 minutes.

Makes about 6 cups.

Steak Sauce

1 cup chopped mushrooms
10 anchovy fillets
3 garlic cloves, minced
1 cup (250 ml) oil

3 cups (750 ml) red wine
½ cup (125 ml) brandy
1 cup tomato paste
½ cup chopped parsley

1. Cook mushrooms, anchovy fillets and garlic in oil for 5 minutes.
2. Add the rest of the ingredients.
3. Bring to boil and reduce to simmer for 15 minutes.

Makes about 6 cups.

Hot Chilli Sauce

1 cup (250 ml) tomato sauce
1 tablespoon chilli powder
½ cup grated onion
½ teaspoon marjoram

½ teaspoon thyme
¼ cup (60 ml) red wine
¼ cup sugar
1 tablespoon cornstarch

Place all ingredients in a saucepan and simmer gently for 15 minutes.

Easy Basting Sauce

3 cups (725 ml) tomato sauce
½ teaspoon dry mustard
½ teaspoon chilli powder
1 small onion, chopped finely
1 garlic clove, crushed
4 dessertspoons treacle
¾ cup vinegar

Mix all ingredients together and simmer for 40 minutes.

Hollandaise Sauce

¾ cup (188 g) unsalted butter
3 large egg yolks
2 tablespoons lemon juice
salt
white pepper

1. Soften the butter in a heavy pan over a low heat until it is just beginning to melt. Set aside and keep warm.
2. Put the egg yolks into a small stainless steel or enamelled saucepan and beat with a whisk for 2 minutes or until they are thick.
3 Put the eggs over in a very low heat and add the butter very slowly. Lift the saucepan off the stove to prevent over-heating every now and again.
·4. As soon as the sauce is thick and creamy, add the lemon juice and salt and pepper to taste.

Apricot Barbecue Sauce

¼ cup vegetable oil
¼ cup vinegar
½ cup apricot nectar
¼ cup mashed apricots
½ cup tomato sauce
1 tablespoon brown sugar

2 tablespoons grated onion
½ teaspoon Worcestershire sauce
1 teaspoon salt
½ teaspoon oregano
dash Tabasco sauce

Combine all ingredients and bring to boil. Simmer gently for 10 minutes.
Serve with beef, pork, lamb, veal, chicken or frankfurters.

Bearnaise Sauce

4 tablespoons tarragon wine
vinegar
3 tablespoons dry white wine
2 tablespoons chopped scallions
or spring onions
1½ tablespoons finely chopped
fresh tarragon
or 2 teaspoons dried tarragon
and 1 tablespoon parsley

¾ cup Hollandaise Sauce
(see recipe made without lemon juice)
salt
white pepper

1. Make the Hollandaise Sauce without the lemon juice and keep warm by standing over some hot water.
2. Mix vinegar, wine, onions and fresh or dried tarragon in a small saucepan and boil quickly until the mixture is reduced to 2 tablespoons.
3. Whisk the strained mixture into the warm Hollandaise Sauce then add the tablespoon parsley.
4. Season with salt and pepper.

Greek Sauce

1 cup chopped tomatoes	1 tablespoon sugar
1 cup (250 ml) dry white wine	1 bay leaf, crumbled
1 cup beef stock	½ teaspoon Tabasco sauce
(made with 2 beef cubes)	½ cup chopped onion
½ cup finely chopped celery	2 cloves garlic, crushed
1 tablespoon lemon juice	1 teaspoon salt
¼ cup Worcestershire sauce	freshly ground black pepper
2 tablespoons oil	

1. Combine all ingredients and bring to boil. Reduce and simmer for 45 minutes.
2. Strain, serve with chicken, ham, pork, frankfurters, lamb.

Curry Butter

3 tablespoons (60 g) butter or table
   margarine
1 tablespoon lemon juice
pinch cayenne pepper
½ teaspoon salt
½ teaspoon freshly ground
   black pepper

1. Cream butter or margarine till soft and light, add lemon juice and seasonings.
2. Turn into waxed paper, shape into cylinder, wrap and chill well.

For seafoods.

Garlic Butter

½ cup (125 g) butter or table
   margarine
1 large crushed clove garlic
2 tablespoons parsley
½ teaspoon salt
½ teaspoon freshly ground
   black pepper

1. Cream butter or margarine well (use electric mixer if possible).
2. Add garlic, parsley and seasonings.
3. Turn into waxed paper, shape into cylinder 1 inch x 1½ inches (3 cm x 4 cm) in diameter and wrap in the paper.
4. Refrigerate until well chilled.
5. To serve slice crosswise into ½ inch (1 cm) pats.

For beef, veal, lamb or hamburgers, also for making garlic bread.

Maitre D'hotel Butter

½ cup (125 g) butter or table
   margarine
2 tablespoons lemon juice
2 tablespoons finely chopped
   parsley

½ teaspoon salt
½ teaspoon freshly ground
   black pepper

1. Cream butter or margarine well (use electric mixer if possible).
2. Add lemon juice, parsley and seasonings.
3. Turn into waxed paper, shape into cylinder 1 inch x 1½ inches (3 cm x 4 cm) in diameter. Wrap in the paper.
4. Refrigerate until well chilled.
5. To serve slice crosswise into ½ inch (1 cm) pats.

For fish, steak, lamb or hamburgers.

Hot Curry Marinade

2 **tablespoons salad oil**
2 **tablespoons vinegar**
1 **teaspoon curry powder**

1. Dissolve curry powder in vinegar, stir in oil.
2. Season meat with salt and pepper and place in marinade and soak for at least 1 hour, at room temperature.
3. Turn meat occasionally.

For beef, pork or lamb.

Chicken Marinade

½ **cup (125 ml) white wine**
½ **cup salad oil**
1 **tablespoon chopped scallions**
   or **chives**
1 **tablespoon chopped parsley**

Season chicken pieces, soak in marinade for at least 30 minutes at room temperature, turning occasionally.

Hawaiian Marinade

½ **cup (125 ml) pineapple juice**   ½ **teaspoon ground ginger**
⅓ **cup oil**   ⅛ **teaspoon ground mace**
¼ **cup soya sauce**   ¼ **cup brown sugar**
1 **tablespoon lemon juice**   3 **tablespoons honey**
1 **teaspoon dry mustard**

1. Mix all ingredients together.
2. This mixture can be used for all barbecue cuts, pork, lamb and lamb shanks for marinating at room temperature for 1 or 2 hours.

Tomato Salad Dressing

1 can (small) tomato soup
¾ of can of sugar
teaspoon salt
freshly ground black pepper
dessertspoon dry mustard
clove garlic, crushed
1 tablespoon Worcestershire sauce
1 cup of paraffin oil
1½ cups of malt vinegar

Mix all ingredients together in a sealed bottle, shake and mix thoroughly.

Blue Cheese Salad Dressing

½ cup blue cheese, crumbled
¼ cup (60 ml) dry white wine
¼ cup sour cream
½ cup cottage cheese
¼ teaspoon salt
dash cayenne pepper
¼ teaspoon powdered caraway
   seed (optional)

Combine all ingredients until smooth and creamy (a blender can be used).
Makes 1 cup.

Sour Cream Mayonnaise

½ cup mayonnaise
½ cup sour cream
1 tablespoon lemon juice
1 teaspoon curry powder
1 tablespoon fresh onion juice

Mix all ingredients together until smooth.

French Style Mayonnaise

4 egg yolks, room temperature
4 teaspoons lemon juice
   or white wine vinegar
½ teaspoon salt
white pepper
1 teaspoon mustard
¾ cup olive oil
boiling water

1. Place egg yolks into a large bowl and stir with a wooden spoon for about three minutes.
2. Add the salt, mustard and pepper.
3. Add the oil now, dropping a little in at a time, until the mixture begins to thicken. Once this is done more can be added a little faster making sure all the oil is absorbed before a little more is added.
4. When all the oil has been used up, the mayonnaise should be stiff and shiny. Taste and season if necessary.
5. Beat in a little boiling water, a teaspoon at a time, until the mayonnaise is a creamy texture.
6. Add the lemon juice or vinegar to taste.

Mayonnaise (Blender Version)

2 eggs
½ cup salad oil
4 tablespoons lemon juice
½ teaspoon salt
½ teaspoon dry mustard
½ teaspoon white pepper
1½ cups salad oil

Place all ingredients in a blender. Cover the container and turn motor on high. Immediately remove the cover and add the 1½ cups of oil slowly pouring it steadily in a thin stream.

Lime and Honey Salad Dressing

¼ cup honey
1 teaspoon salt
1 teaspoon mustard
1 tablespoon paprika

¼ cup lemon or lime juice
1 cup olive oil
2 tablespoons onion juice

1. Put honey, salt, mustard, paprika and lemon juice into a saucepan and bring to boil.
2. Cool and add the other ingredients and beat with either a rotary beater or better still in the electric blender.
3. Serve over green salad.

Wine Vinegar Dressing

3 tablespoons white
   or red wine vinegar
salt, pepper
½ teaspoon dry mustard
8 tablespoons olive oil
½ teaspoon sugar

1. Beat the vinegar with the salt, pepper, mustard and sugar.
2. Add the oil a drop at a time beating continually until the oil is completely absorbed. Taste and if necessary season.

Lemon juice may be used instead of the wine vinegar.

Coconut Milk

¾ cup desiccated coconut
1 cup (250 ml) water
   or 1 cup (250 ml) milk for a
   richer coconut milk
pinch salt

1. Place coconut, water, or milk and salt in a small saucepan and bring slowly to simmering point.
2. Strain through a fine sieve into a basin pressing coconut firmly with the back of a spoon to extract more milk.

Hors d'œuvres and First Courses

Spiced Yoghurt Dip

1 x 4 oz (125 g) package cream
  cheese, softened
1 x 6½ oz (200 g) carton
  apricot yoghurt
1 teaspoon curry powder
½ cup desiccated coconut
½ teaspoon salt

1. Blend cream cheese until smooth and add the yoghurt beating lightly.
2. Stir in the curry powder, coconut and salt and let stand for several hours to thicken in refrigerator.
3. Spoon into serving bowl and sprinkle top with a little curry powder and garnish edge with a wedge of apple or pineapple.

This dip is nice served with bite-size pieces of apple, melon, fresh pineapple, mango, peaches or tangerine segments.

Pineapple and Walnut Dip

4 oz (125 g) package cream
   cheese
1 tablespoon crushed,
   drained pineapple
1 tablespoon chopped walnuts

1. Bring cream cheese to room temperature and beat until smooth.
2. Add all other ingredients and sufficient milk to make the mixture a dip-ping consistency.
3. Chill for at least an hour in the refrigerator and serve in a small bowl with potato chips and crackers.

Smoked Oyster Dip

4 oz (125 g) package cream
   cheese
1 can smoked oysters (drained)
1 teaspoon lemon juice
salt
freshly ground black pepper
milk

1. Bring cream cheese to room temperature and beat until smooth.
2. Add all other ingredients and sufficient milk to make the mixture a dip-ping consistency.
3. Chill for at least 1 hour and serve in small bowl with potato chips and crackers.

Onion Dip

    4 oz (125 g) package
      cream cheese
    ½ teaspoon salt
    pinch cayenne pepper
    3 dessertspoons spring onions

1. Bring cream cheese to room temperature and beat until smooth.
2. Add all other ingredients and sufficient milk to make the mixture a dipping consistency.
3. Chill for at least 1 hour in the refrigerator and serve in a small bowl with potato chips and crackers.

Mock Pate

    1 small liverwurst sausage
    ¼ cup finely chopped onion
    1 teaspoon mustard
    ½ cup heavy sour cream
    ½ cup finely chopped parsley
    salt
    freshly ground pepper
    ¼ cup brandy

1. Mash the liverwurst thoroughly with the onion, mustard, sour cream, parsley, salt, pepper and brandy.
2. Place in a bowl and leave in the refrigerator for at least 1 hour.

Serve on small crackers or small fried croutons.

Garlic Olives

**bottled, canned green
   olives
garlic
lemon
oil**

1. Cover olives with olive oil, in a bottle.
2. Add sliced cloves of garlic and a few slices of lemon. Let stand for at least 24 hours.

Cheese Chips

**package of potato chips
Parmesan or cheddar cheese
paprika *or* onion salt**

1. Sprinkle potato chips generously with the grated Parmesan or cheddar cheese, paprika or onion salt and pepper.
2. Bake in a moderate oven, until brown and crisp.

Serve hot or cold.

Beef Consomme

**1 can condensed beef
   consomme
sour cream
chives**

1. Chill consomme in the can overnight in the refrigerator. The consomme should be a jelly consistency.
2. Spoon carefully into individual soup bowls and serve topped with sour cream and snipped chives.

A lovely cool starter for a warm day.

Serves 4.

Cream of Lettuce Soup

2 large heads of lettuce	¼ cup flour
1 medium sized onion, finely chopped	3¾ cups (900 ml) milk freshly chopped mint
2 tablespoons (40 g) butter *or* table margarine	2 egg yolks ½ cup cream

1. Cut the lettuce finely.
2. Melt the butter and add the lettuce and onion, cover and stew gently for 6 minutes. Take from heat and mix in the flour.
3. Bring the milk to the boil and pour in mixing all the time.
4. Add salt and pepper to taste and return to heat.
5. Simmer for 20 minutes and blend in a blender or put through and sieve.
6. Check the seasoning again and sprinkle with freshly chopped mint.
7. Return to the heat and add a mixture of the eggs and cream. Bring nearly to boiling point.
8. Transfer to a bowl and when cooled leave in refrigerator for several hours to chill. Preferably overnight to bring out the flavor.

Serves 6.

Avocado with Iced Turtle Soup

2 tablespoons gelatin	lemon juice
1 can (500 ml) clear turtle soup	sour cream
¾ can water	caviar
dry sherry	2 large avocados

1. Cut avocados in half, remove seed and squeeze a little lemon juice over to stop browning.
2. Dissolve gelatin in water and mix with turtle soup.
3. Fill the empty can with ¾ water and dry sherry and lemon juice in equal quantities. Mix with the rest of the soup and chill in a bowl until set.
4. Spoon into centers of avocados and dot sour cream topped with caviar on top.

This soup is delicious served on its own in individual bowls and topped with sour cream and caviar.

Serves 4.

Cream of Cucumber Soup

1½ pts (750 ml) white stock
  (4 chicken cubes to
  1 pt (500 ml)
2 large cucumbers, peeled and
  cut into wedges
1 large onion, chopped
2 tablespoons (40 g) butter
  or table margarine

¼ cup flour
salt
freshly ground black pepper
fresh or dried mint
2 egg yolks
½ cup cream

1. Cook the cucumber in the stock with the chopped onion for 20 minutes.
2. Blend in the blender or rub through a sieve.
3. Make a mixture of melted butter and flour and cook for 1 minute.
4. Slowly add the blended mixture to the flour mixing quickly so the mixture becomes smooth. Cook until thickened.
5. Cool a little and add a mixture of the beaten egg yolks and cream. Heat gently until the mixture becomes thick once again. Do not boil.
6. Add the chopped fresh or dried mint and allow to cool. Chill in refrigerator for at least 2 hours.

Serves 6.

Chilled Pea Soup with Mint

½ cup (125 ml) cream
1 package frozen peas
1 small onion
1 cup (250 ml) water

salt
freshly ground black pepper
3 cups (750 ml) chicken broth
2 tablespoons flour

1. Cook peas, onion, water, salt and pepper.
2. Add ½ cup chicken broth with flour, mix until smooth.
3. Add balance of broth and heat.
4. Blend peas and broth in a blender or press peas through strainer or food mill and add to broth.
5. Bring to boil.
6. Remove from heat and add ½ cup cream and chill.
7. Before serving add some finely chopped mint.

Excellent served hot too.
Serves 6.

Cold Chicken Senegalese Soup

2 cans condensed cream of
   chicken soup
2 cups light cream
2 tablespoons curry powder
½ cup lemon juice
1 teaspoon salt
freshly ground black pepper
sour cream
chopped chives and parsley

1. Combine chicken soup and cream in a saucepan and stir until smooth and well blended.
2. Mix curry powder with ¼ cup of water and add to soup mixture.
3. Simmer over low heat for 10 minutes stirring frequently.
4. Remove from heat and stir in lemon juice, salt and pepper.
5. Cool for 30 minutes and then chill in refrigerator for at least 1 hour.
6. Serve with a dob of sour cream and chopped chives and parsley sprinkled on top.

Serves 6.

The soup is also delicious when served with chopped green apples sprinkled on top.

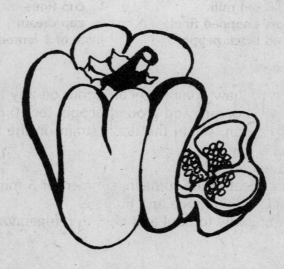

Cream of Potato Soup (Vichyssoise)

3 large leeks, blanched
or 3 large onions
2 tablespoons (40 g) butter
1 stick celery, sliced
4 medium sized potatoes,
thinly sliced

3¾ cups (900 ml) chicken stock
½ cup heavy cream
2 egg yolks, beaten

1. Slice leeks or onions.
2. Soften them in butter, do not brown.
3. Add celery and potatoes and stock.
4. Cook until soft.
5. Blend in a blender or rub through a sieve.
6. Adjust the seasoning and add cream and beaten egg yolks, mixed together. Cook for 2 minutes but do not boil.
7. Allow to cool and chill for at least 2 hours.

Serves 6.

Quick Cream of Spinach Soup

1 small package frozen
spinach purée
1½ pints (750 ml) milk
1 small onion, chopped finely
freshly ground black pepper
salt

nutmeg
2 tablespoons (40 g) butter
½ cup flour
½ cup cream
juice of 1 lemon

1. Allow spinach to thaw completely and pour off any liquid.
2. Simmer milk with onions and ground pepper for 10 minutes.
3. Melt butter in a pan, stir in the flour, strain on the flavored milk and stir until smooth boiling.
4. Simmer for 3 minutes.
5. Take aside and beat in the spinach, simmer for 5 minutes.
6. Season and add lemon juice and nutmeg.
7. Add cream and allow to cool and chill in refrigerator for at least 2 hours.

Serve 6.

Cold Plum Soup

3 lb (1½ kg) red plums
6 cups (1½ liters) chicken stock
2 tablespoons fine tapioca
   or thicken with a little cornstarch
2 cups (500 ml) white wine
¼ cup sugar

½ teaspoon cloves
½ teaspoon cinnamon
1 lemon sliced and seeded
¾ cup slivered almonds
salt and pepper

1. Boil 2 cups of chicken stock and add tapioca, stirring to prevent sticking. Cook until the tapioca is transparent.
2. In another saucepan add washed and steamed plums, the rest of the stock, wine, sugar, cloves, cinnamon and sliced lemon.
3. Cook for 20 minutes or until plums are tender.
4. Draw aside and remove the plum stones. Combine both mixtures and blend in a blender or put through a sieve.
5. Chill for several hours and serve sprinkled with almonds.

Serves 6.

Watercress Soup

2 bunches of watercress
1 medium onion, finely chopped
2 tablespoons (40 g) butter
   or table margarine
¼ cup flour

1½ pts (750 ml) milk
freshly chopped mint
2 egg yolks
½ cup cream
juice of 1 lemon

1. Cut the watercress up finely or break up.
2. Melt the butter or margarine and add the onion, watercress, cover and let stew gently for 6 minutes. Take from heat and mix in the flour.
3. Add boiling milk to the watercress and onion stew, mixing all the time. Add salt and pepper to taste.
4. Simmer for 20 minutes and blend in a blender or put through a sieve.
5. Return to heat and add a mixture of the eggs and cream. Bring nearly to boiling point. Add lemon juice to taste.
6. Transfer to a bowl and when cooled leave in refrigerator for several hours to chill. Preferably overnight to bring out the flavor.

Gazpacho

2 cloves garlic, crushed	1 onion, chopped
2 slices white bread, remove crusts	2 sprigs parsley, chopped
¼ cup olive oil	1 teaspoon fresh or dried basil
8 medium ripe tomatoes	½ teaspoon salt
1 green pepper, seeded and chopped	2 tablespoons vinegar
1 cucumber, skinned and chopped	¾ cup (187½ ml) iced water
	½ cup (125 ml) dry white wine, chilled

1. Pour oil over bread and add the garlic, leave stand for several hours.
2. Combine the bread and all other ingredients, except for iced water and wine, blend in small lots in a blender or put through a sieve.
3. Chill thoroughly for several hours.
4. Before serving add ice water and wine and add 2 iceblocks to keep soup cold while eating. Garnish with chopped cucumber.

Serves 6-8.

Vegetables and Salads

Boiled Asparagus

2 or 3 bunches asparagus
10 pints (5 liters) salted water

1. Tie asparagus together in their bunches with string and cut about ½ inch (1 cm) from the bottom.
2. Bring the salted water to the boil and add asparagus horizontally keeping the water at boiling point. Reduce and leave uncovered for about 30 minutes or until the butt ends are tender. Do not overcook.
3. Serve hot with melted butter, lemon juice and parsley, or Hollandaise Sauce. Also if chilled delicious served with Wine Vinegar Dressing or Mayonnaise (see recipes).

Serves 4 to 6.

Zucchinis

zucchinis
butter or margarine
salt
pepper
1 onion, finely chopped
fresh or dried dill

1. Cut the stalks off the zucchinis and place on a double piece of aluminum foil (approximately 4 zucchinis on each piece).
2. Dot with butter, and sprinkle with salt, freshly ground black pepper and the dill.
3. Seal the foil tightly and barbecue over the fire for about 10 minutes each side.

Boiled Zucchinis

zucchinis
1 medium onion
bay leaf
2 teaspoons dill,
   dried or fresh
salt and pepper

1. Wash and remove stalks from the zucchinis.
2. Boil salted water and add 1 medium onion, bay leaf, dill, freshly ground black pepper or peppercorns.
3. Add zucchinis and bring back to the boil. Turn heat down, cover and let simmer for 7 minutes. Drain immediately.

Delicious served with Wine Vinegar Dressing when chilled (see recipe).

Beet Mold

1 large can beets
cinnamon
2 tablespoons gelatin

1. Drain and keep juice from the can of beets.
2. Place the beets into an oiled mold.
3. Dissolve the gelatin in a cup of cold water. Place over boiling water until gelatin is completely dissolved.
4. Add the gelatin mixture to the juice then sprinkle about ½ teaspoon cinnamon and mix well.
5. Pour the mixture gently over the beets and chill in refrigerator until set.

Serves 6-8.

Beets in their Jackets

4 large raw beets
sour cream
chives or parsley

1. Take off the tails and tops of beets and put into hot oven for approximately 1 hour.
2. Serve topped with sour cream and parsley or chives.

Butter is also delicious added to the beets.

Boiled Artichokes

6 artichokes	peppercorns
onion	oil
bay leaf	1 teaspoon sugar
basil or dill	1 tablespoon lemon juice
salt	

1. Wash artichokes and cut off their stalks up to ½ inch (1 cm) from the globe.
2. Cover the artichokes with water, add the rest of the ingredients and bring to the boil.
3. Reduce the heat and simmer with the lid on for 35 to 40 minutes.
4. Serve the artichokes with hot melted butter, lemon and parsley mixed, or Hollandaise Sauce. If cold, serve with Wine Vinegar Dressing or Oil Mayonnaise (see recipes).

Serves 6.

Herbed Tomatoes

⅔ cup salad oil	½ teaspoon coarse black pepper
¼ cup vinegar	6 whole peeled tomatoes
½ teaspoon dried basil	⅓ cup chopped parsley
1 teaspoon salt	⅓ cup chopped chives

1. Combine salad oil, vinegar, basil, salt and pepper.
2. Place tomatoes in a shallow bowl and pour dressing over.
3. Chill 2 or 3 hours turning tomatoes occasionally.
4. Remove from dressing, roll in parsley and chives.

Serves 6.

Herbed Scalloped Tomatoes

4 cups tomatoes
2 tablespoons sugar
1 teaspoon salt
½ teaspoon nutmeg
½ teaspoon pepper
½ teaspoon basil

Stuffing:
2 cups breadcrumbs
1 cup finely chopped onion
pepper
salt
teaspoon mixed herbs

1. Prepare the stuffing by frying onions until brown in two tablespoons fat. Combine with crumbs etc.
2. Mix with tomatoes and seasonings in buttered casserole, reserving about ⅓ stuffing for the top.
3. Dot with butter.
4. Bake in moderate oven 375°F (190°C) for 45 minutes.

Serves 4-6.

Tomato Puff

2 cups canned tomatoes
1½ cups soft breadcrumbs
¾ cup grated sharp cheese
1 teaspoon salt
3 beaten egg yolks
3 beaten egg whites

1. Mix first 5 ingredients together then fold in stiffly beaten egg whites.
2. Bake for 45 minutes at 350°F (180°C).

Serves 4-6.

Tomatoes

4 large ripe tomatoes	1 can (470 g) baked beans
3 tablespoons vinegar	in tomato sauce
1 tablespoon chopped onion	1 teaspoon Worcestershire sauce
¼ cup grated or chopped	2 tablespoons parsley
blue vein cheese	

1. Cut tomatoes into quarters, but not all the way through.
2. Mix all the remaining ingredients together and fill the tomatoes.
3. Place each tomato on a small piece of aluminum foil sufficient to hold the tomatoes and stuffing together. Fold around tomatoes.
4. Barbecue over coals for 15 minutes or until done.
5. Remove aluminum foil and barbecue again for 3 minutes until brown.

Serves 4.

These may be served grilled or served chilled.

Tomato Aspic

3 cups tomato juice	⅛ teaspoon pepper
1 stalk celery	2½ tablespoons gelatin
1 sliced small onion	1½ tablespoons sugar
2 lemon slices	⅔ cup cold tomato juice
1 bay leaf	¼ cup vinegar
1 teaspoon salt	dash of Worcestershire sauce

1. Combine tomato juice, celery, lemon, onion, bay leaf, salt, pepper, sugar and Worcestershire sauce, and simmer uncovered for 10 minutes. Strain and set aside.
2. Soften gelatin in cold juice and vinegar, then stir into strained mixture.
3. Pour into mold and refrigerate until firm.

Delicious served broken up into pieces and placed in soup bowls with a dob of sour cream and chives on top.

Serves 6-8.

Boston Beans

2 cans (445 g) baked beans in
  tomato sauce
½ lb (250 g) bacon
2 tablespoons molasses
1 large onion, chopped
1 tablespoon parsley,
  chopped

1. Soften onion in a little butter in a heavy pan.
2. Add the bacon and crisp.
3. Mix in the baked beans, chopped parsley and molasses.
4. Cover and cook for about 1 hour over low heat.

This is delicious served with all cuts of barbecued meat.

Stuffed Green Peppers

8 green peppers
1½ cups cooked rice
3 large chopped tomatoes
salt
freshly ground pepper
½ teaspoon basil
paprika

1. Cut and slice the stem end of the peppers and remove the seeds and white ribs.
2. Place on a double thickness of heavy duty aluminum foil.
3. Fill the peppers with the mixture of cooked rice, chopped tomatoes, salt, pepper, basil and sprinkle with paprika. Grated cheese may also be added at the top.
4. Wrap securely in the foil and barbecue for about 30 minutes. Turn once during barbecue.

Serves 8.

Cheese Corn Cobs

  4 **frozen corn cobs**
  3 **tablespoons butter**
    or **margarine, softened**
  ½ **cup grated Parmesan cheese**
  1 **tablespoon chopped parsley**
  4 **slices pastrami**
    (*or* **bacon slices**)

1. Thaw the corn and dry thoroughly.
2. Beat together butter, cheese and parsley until blended. Spread evenly over each corn cob leaving about ¾ inch (2 cm) at each end.
3. Roll pastrami slices around each cob and seal each in a piece of aluminum foil. Prick the foil well to allow moisture to escape.
4. Cook on barbecue for about 10 minutes each side.

Serves 4.

Sweet Corn

  corn
  salt
  freshly ground black pepper

1. Choose tender sweet corn in the husks. Strip husks down to the end but do not tear off. Remove the silk.
2. Let the corn stand in iced water for 20 minutes to 1 hour, then drain well.
3. Brush corn with softened butter or margarine and sprinkle with salt and freshly ground pepper.
4. Bring husks up around the corn. Be sure entire ear is covered.
5. Wrap each ear securely in a double thickness of heavy duty aluminum foil making sure it is well sealed.
6. Barbecue for about 15 minutes on each side.

Herbed Potatoes

4 medium sized potatoes,
peeled and sliced thinly
½ cup (125 g) melted butter
  or margarine
1 tablespoon chopped parsley

1 tablespoon snipped chives
½ teaspoon dried basil
½ teaspoon salt
freshly ground black pepper

1. Put potato slices into a bowl, add melted butter or margarine, herbs, salt, and pepper, stir to coat the slices.
2. Wrap securely in two layers of aluminum foil and cook on the barbecue turning regularly for 20 minutes or until done.

Serves 4.

Baked Potatoes in Foil

potatoes
butter
sour cream
chopped chives
Parmesan cheese

1. Scrub potatoes with stiff brush and cut out any large eyes.
2. Wrap in single layer of foil and bake on the grill until tender.
3. Serve by slashing across the foil and potatoes with a cross. Open and let steam escape and serve with pats of butter and a bowl of sour cream, chopped chives and Parmesan cheese to taste.

Ratatouille

2 large onions, sliced	1 lb (500 g) tomatoes
2 cloves garlic, chopped	1 teaspoon dill, fresh or dried
½ cup olive oil	1 teaspoon basil
2 small eggplants, peeled and cubed	1 teaspoon salt
6 small zucchinis, sliced	1 teaspoon parsley
2 green peppers, cut in strips	freshly ground black pepper
1 head fennel, sliced	

1. Heat the oil in a pan. Soften onions and garlic in pan. Add eggplant, zucchini, peppers, fennel and mix well over heat.
2. Mix in the tomatoes and seasonings.
3. Cover and simmer for about 1 hour, stirring regularly.
4. Remove cover and allow liquid to be evaporated and the mixture thicken.
5. Serve hot or cold.

Serves 6.

Marinated Cucumber

1 cucumber
soya sauce
vinegar
salad oil

1. Peel and slice cucumber or leave unpeeled for easier digestion.
2. Marinate in equal parts of soya sauce, vinegar and salad oil. No salt.

Baked Onions

onions
salt
freshly ground black pepper
sugar

1. Skin onions and sprinkle with salt, pepper and a little sugar.
2. Wrap in foil and place over barbecue. Bake slowly until tender (about 1 hour).

Baked Mushrooms

6 **medium sized mushrooms
per person**
2 **tablespoons (40 g) butter**
or **margarine**
salt
freshly ground black pepper

1. Place mushrooms in a square of doubled, heavy duty, aluminum foil.
2. Add butter or margarine, few grains of salt and freshly ground pepper.
3. Wrap foil tightly around mushrooms and barbecue for about 4 minutes, turn and cook 4 minutes longer.

Sweet Cole Slaw

½ **cup mayonnaise**
1 **tablespoon lemon juice**
2 **teaspoons prepared mustard**
1 **teaspoon salt**
3 **cups shredded cabbage**
1 **cup grated carrot**
½ **cup raisins**
½ **cup chopped walnuts**

Combine the first four ingredients and mix with vegetables and raisins, toss lightly.

4-6 Servings.

Raisins are improved if "plumped" in a streamer over hot water and then chilled.

Salade Nicoise

1 head of lettuce
½ lb (250 g) green beans
½ lb (250 g) new potatoes
finely chopped parsley
2 hard boiled eggs
1 small can tuna
½ cup black olives
1 can anchovies
1 medium onion, sliced
½ lb (250 g) tomatoes

1. Cut lettuce into quarters.
2. Cut beans into 1 inch (2½ cm) pieces, cook in a little salted boiling water until just tender, drain.
3. Boil potatoes and slice thickly.
4. Shell and quarter eggs.
5. Flake tuna.
6. Stone olives.
7. Drain anchovies.
8. Slice onion.
9. Quarter tomatoes.
10. Arrange ingredients in layers in a bowl beginning with beans and potatoes at bottom, tuna and tomatoes next, eggs and lettuce next and dot with olives, anchovies, parsley and slices of onion.
11. Pour over vinaigrette dressing just before serving.

Serves 6-8.

Cole Slaw

**the heart of one medium
    cabbage**
2 stalks celery
4 spring onions
    or **one medium onion**

1. Finely shred vegetables.
2. Mix well and chill thoroughly.
3. Sprinkle with salt and moisten lightly with a sharp mayonnaise.

Mayonnaise:
1 can condensed milk
red wine vinegar
    or **sharp malt vinegar**
2 teaspoons prepared hot mustard
salt
freshly ground black pepper

4. Mix vinegar with condensed milk until it thickens and is sharp to taste.
5. Add the mustard, salt and pepper to taste.

Serves 6-8.

Caesar Salad

2 heads lettuce	6 tablespoons oil
1 bunch spring onions	(salad, peanut or soya)
chives	2 tablespoons lemon juice or vinegar
celery or watercress	or a mixture of both
¼ teaspoon dry mustard	½ cup grated cheese
½ teaspoon salt	1 egg
freshly ground black pepper	2 cups croutons

1. Rub bowl with 1 clove of garlic. Add mustard, salt, pepper, then mix in blended oil and vinegar. Mix well and add washed and dried greens.
2. Add grated cheese and raw egg, and toss until each leaf is well coated and egg disappears.
3. Toss croutons in a pan with hot butter until they are crisp and brown and add to salad at last minute.

Serves 4-6.

Ham Salad

2 cups cooked ham,	mayonnaise
cut into 1 inch (2½ cm) cubes	1 head lettuce
½ cup celery, chopped	3 hard-boiled eggs
1 onion, chopped	finely chopped parsley
½ cup chutney or sweet pickle	1 teaspoon chopped dill

1. Mix ham with celery, onion, chutney and mayonnaise.
2. Place on lettuce leaves and surround by quartered eggs and sprinkle with parsley and dill.

Serves 4-6.

Sausage with Potato Salad

1 lb (500 g) uncooked garlic
    (Polish, French or Italian) sausage
3 lb (1½ kg) firm potatoes cut into
    ¼ inch (1 cm) slices
boiling salted water
3 tablespoons chicken stock
3 tablespoons white wine vinegar
½ teaspoon dry mustard

10 tablespoons olive oil
2 tablespoons grated onion
1 tablespoon chives
½ teaspoon dry dill
2 tablespoons chopped green pepper
3 slices bacon, rind removed,
    diced and fried crisp
3 tablespoons fresh parsley

1. Pierce the sausages in 6 places with a fork to prevent the skin from bursting.
2. Bring sausages to boil in a saucepan just with water covering the sausages and simmer for 40 minutes.
3. Transfer the sausages to kitchen paper to drain and cool.
4. Peel the skin off the sausages.
5. While the sausages are cooking, cover the potatoes with salted boiling water and cook for 12 minutes or until the potatoes are just done, but do not overcook.
6. Drain thoroughly and place in a large bowl.
7. Heat the chicken stock and pour over the warm potatoes tossing them very gently a couple of times.
8. Allow to stand for some minutes until the stock is completely absorbed.
9. Mix vinegar, salt and dry mustard together in a bowl and add to the potatoes and allow them to stand for a few more minutes to absorb the seasoning.
10. Pour in the oil and sprinkle in the onions, chives, dill, green pepper, crispy bacon and parsley and turn the potatoes to coat them with the oil and herbs.
11. Serve the warm potato salad from a bowl or dish with the sausage sliced into ½ inch (1 cm) slices arranged around it.

Serves 4 to 6 people.

This potato salad is nice chilled.

Crunchy Potato Salad

1½ lb (750 g) cooked potatoes
3 hard boiled eggs
¾ teaspoon salt
½ teaspoon pepper
½ teaspoon celery seeds
½ cup diced cucumber
½ cup diced celery
½ cup chopped onion

½ cup diced sweet pickle
(optional)
¼ cup grated carrot
¾ cup salad dressing
  or mayonnaise
2 tablespoons prepared mustard
and vinegar

1. Coarsely dice potatoes and eggs and sprinkle with salt, pepper and celery seeds.
2. Add diced, pared cucumber, celery, onion, pickle and carrot.
3. Mix salad dressing with mustard and vinegar and pour over potato mixture. Toss until well coated adding more mayonnaise if necessary. Refrigerate.

Served 6-8.

Dice potatoes before cooking for easier handling.
Crumbled crispy bacon is a good addition.

Hot Bacon Potato Salad

6 slices bacon
½ cup chopped onions
1 teaspoon salt
1 tablespoon sugar
1 tablespoon flour
1 teaspoon celery seed
dash of pepper
¾ cup (187½ ml) water

¼ cup vinegar
4 cups sliced cooked potato
½ cup chopped celery
2 hard-boiled eggs, quartered
8 cherry tomatoes, halved
  or 4 large tomatoes, quartered
1 cup small spinach leaves

1. Fry bacon until crisp. Remove from pan and pour off all but ¼ cup fat.
2. Add onion and cook until lightly browned, stirring.
3. Stir in next 6 ingredients. Add water and vinegar and cook stirring until thickened.
4. Add potato and celery, mix lightly and heat gently.
5. Add eggs, tomatoes, spinach leaves and crumbled bacon.
6. Let stand over heat until warmed through.

Serves 4 to 6.

Tomato and Cucumber Salad

tomatoes
cucumber

Russian Dressing:
1 cup salad oil
½ cup tomato sauce
⅓ cup vinegar
2 tablespoons salt
freshly ground black pepper
1 teaspoon grated onion

1. Wash tomatoes and slice not quite through to stem end.
2. Slice unpeeled cucumber very thinly and place slices in each split of tomato.
3. Make Russian Dressing by combining ingredients in order listed. Serve over the tomatoes.

Serves 6-8.

Avocado and Apple Salad

1 large avocado
1 large green apple
1 tablespoon halved salted
   peanuts
salad dressing

1. Peel and slice avocado and green apples. Place in a large bowl and mix carefully with salted peanuts.
2. Pour over salad dressing a little at a time until the mixture is completely covered, but not too much.
3. Serve in a small bowl as either a salad or a summer starter.

Serves 4.

Cucumber and Yoghurt Salad

4 cucumbers, peeled and cut
    into quarters lengthwise
1 teaspoon salt
2 cloves garlic, minced
2 tablespoons lemon juice
2 cups yoghurt
1 tablespoon chopped mint
1 teaspoon salt
¼ cup oil
mint for garnishing

1. Sprinkle cucumbers with salt and drain well.
2. Mix garlic, lemon juice, yoghurt and mint and add to cucumbers.
3. Pour oil over the top and garnish with mint.

Serves 6.

Mushroom Salad

2 cups mushrooms, sliced
2 cups watercress,
    washed and chopped
½ cup (125 ml) French dressing
salt and pepper

1. Mix mushrooms and watercress lightly together. Pour over French dressing
    and season to taste.

Serves 6.

Cucumber Salad

3 cucumbers
juice of 1 lemon
salt and pepper
2-3 tablespoons fresh cream
chopped parsley

1. Peel the cucumbers and cut them into large chunks. Plunge them into boiling water for 1 minute, allow them to cool, and when cold add the cream and lemon juice. Season with salt and pepper.
2. Mix well and sprinkle with chopped parsley.
3. Chill for at least 30 minutes.

For variation finely snipped chives or spring onions can be added.

Serves 6.

Curried Rice Salad

1½ cups cooked rice
½ cup chopped onions
1 tablespoon vinegar
2 tablespoons salad oil
1 teaspoon curry powder
1 cup chopped celery
2 cups cooked green peas
1 cup salad dressing

1. Mix rice, onion, vinegar, salad oil and curry powder and refrigerate for 3 hours.
2. Add celery, peas and salad dressing to rice and serve on lettuce leaves.

Serves 6.

This can be pressed into a mold and when chilled turned onto a large platter.

Egg Salad

6 hard-boiled eggs, quartered
1 cup celery, cut on angle
2 tablespoons minced green pepper
1 teaspoon minced onion
¼ cup mayonnaise
½ teaspoon Worcestershire sauce
dash Tabasco

1 tablespoon vinegar
¼ teaspoon salt
¼ teaspoon pepper
3 strips of bacon, fried crisply
   and crumbled
2 olives, chopped

1. Cut eggs into large pieces and chill.
2. Mix the eggs with other ingredients and serve.

Serves 6.

Crispy Egg Salad

2 cucumbers, peeled and cut
   into thin slices
6 hard-boiled eggs, quartered
2 green peppers, seeded and sliced
¾ cup black olives
½ cup olive oil

salt
freshly ground black pepper
pinch of dry mustard
1 teaspoon paprika
3 tablespoons wine vinegar

1. Put cucumbers into a bowl and sprinkle with salt and leave for 15 minutes. Dry and arrange in bottom of serving dish.
2. Place quartered eggs on top and make a border of sliced green peppers on top of the eggs.
3. Scatter around the black olives.
4. Mix oil and seasonings and add vinegar.
5. Pour over the salad.
6. Let stand for at least 30 minutes before serving.

Serves 4.

Marinated Mushrooms Greek Style

3 cups (750 ml) chicken stock
1 cup (125 ml) dry white wine
1 cup olive oil
6 tablespoons lemon juice
6 sprigs of parsley
2 large cloves garlic, cut up
½ teaspoon dried thyme
10 peppercorns

1 teaspoon salt
1 teaspoon mustard, dry
1 lb (500 g) mushrooms,
   sliced if large
freshly ground black pepper
2 tablespoons chopped parsley
2 lemons, cut in thin slices

1. Mix all the ingredients except mushrooms, parsley and lemon slices together in a large enamelled or stainless steel saucepan.
2. Bring to boil, partially cover the saucepan and simmer slowly for 50 minutes.
3. Strain the marinade into a large bowl.
4. Return the marinade to the saucepan and bring to the boil then turn it down to simmering point.
5. Drop in the mushrooms, cover the pan and simmer for 10 minutes.
6. Strain the mushrooms keeping the marinade and transfer carefully to a shallow dish.
7. Taste the marinade and season if necessary, then pour it over the mushrooms.
8. Place the dish in the refrigerator and chill for at least 4 hours.
9. To serve lift the mushrooms out of the marinade and arrange on a serving dish. Moisten the mushrooms with a little marinade, sprinkle them with parsley and garnish with lemon slices.

Serves 6.

Apple and Celery Salad

Dressing:
8 tablespoons oil
4 tablespoons wine vinegar
2 level teaspoons Dijon mustard
1 tablespoon chopped onion
1 tablespoon chopped parsley
freshly ground black pepper

Salad:
2 heads green celery
3 oz (90 g) walnuts
5 red eating apples

1. Make the dressing by placing all ingredients in a screw topped jar and shaking well. Chill for 30 minutes.
2. Trim the ends off the celery and split up into sticks. Wash and cut into thin julienne strips about 2 inches (5 cm) long. Cut the walnuts in small pieces and place in a bowl with the celery.
3. Core the apples and cut into cubes. Add the celery and nuts. Pour enough of the chilled dressing over to moisten, then fork through.

Serves 4-6.

Mango Salad

mangoes
fresh pineapple chunks
oil and vinegar dressing
salt
freshly ground black pepper
1 teaspoon sugar

1. Peel, seed and slice mangoes and add an equal quantity of fresh pineapple chunks.
2. Mix lightly in oil and vinegar dressing. Add a little sugar to taste.

A lovely addition to the Barbecue Table.

Apples

corn syrup
large green apples
brown sugar
cinnamon
nutmeg
raisins

1. Core the apples and pare a third of the way down from the stem end.
2. Fill the centers with a mixture of the brown sugar, cinnamon, nutmeg and raisins.
3. Brush the peeled surface with the corn syrup and put about ½ teaspoon of butter or margarine on each.
4. Wrap securely in the aluminum foil.
5. Barbecue 1 hour on the grill until the apples are done.

Orange Salad

3 large oranges, peeled
and sliced
finely chopped mint
¼ cup oil
2 tablespoons lemon juice
1 teaspoon coconut (desiccated)
1 tablespoon brandy

1. Place the peeled oranges overlapping on a plate with mint and coconut sprinkled on top.
2. Combine the oil and lemon juice and brandy and pour over the oranges.
3. Chill for several hours.

Serves 4.

Fruit Salad with Orange Dressing

fruit salad
¾ cup olive oil
1 teaspoon salt
1 tablespoon vinegar
¼ cup lemon juice
1 tablespoon catsup

2 tablespoons orange juice
or pineapple juice
2 tablespoons honey
2 cloves of garlic

1. Mix all the ingredients well and let the sliced cloves of garlic stand in the dressing for at least 2 hours.
2. Pour over the fruit salad.

This is a delicious addition to the Barbecue Table.

Honey Grilled Pineapple and Mangoes

1 medium sized pineapple
1 mango
4 tablespoons honey
1 tablespoon (20 g) butter or margarine

1. Cut the pineapple and mango into long slices.
2. Place a slice of pineapple and mango on a double thickness of aluminum foil.
3. Pour honey over each and allow to stand at room temperature for at least 1 hour.
4. Dot each of the slices with a little butter or margarine and wrap securely.
5. Barbecue for at least 15 minutes.

Serves 4-6.

Peach Kebab

6 **canned peach halves, drained**
3 **bananas, thickly sliced**
2 **apples, thickly sliced**
1 **fresh pineapple, thickly sliced**
1 **cup (250 ml) grapefruit juice**
1 **cup honey**
3 **tablespoons Cointreau**
1 **teaspoon chopped mint**

1. Mix grapefruit juice, honey, Cointreau and mint together.
2. Marinate peaches, bananas, apples, and pineapple in the mixture for at least 30 minutes at room temperature.
3. Thread onto skewers alternating the fruits.
4. Cook over barbecue for about 5 minutes basting with marinade.

Serves 6.

Spiced Bananas

bananas
lemon juice
butter or margarine
brown sugar
cinnamon, nutmeg or mace

1. Peel bananas and place on a double thickness of heavy duty aluminum foil.
2. Brush with lemon juice and sprinkle generously with brown sugar, dust with cinnamon, nutmeg or mace or the three spices.
3. Dot with butter or margarine and wrap foil securely around the bananas sealing tightly.
4. Barbecue for 9 minutes.

Meats, Poultry and Seafoods

Bacon and Beef Meat Loaf

2 lb (1 kg) ground beef round
  (finely ground)
1 onion, grated
4 bacon slices, finely chopped
½ cup dry breadcrumbs
2 eggs
½ cup (125 ml) canned
  condensed tomato soup

1. Mix together all ingredients except tomato and Worcestershire sauce.
2. Shape firmly into long loaf and place on greased aluminum foil, wrapping it around the sides of the loaf but not closing it at the top.
3. Cook over barbecue turning it over several times.
4. When cooked remove aluminum foil and crisp on the outside basting it with the tomato and Worcestershire sauce.

Serves 4-6.

Western Meat Loaf

1 lb (500 g) ground beef
½ lb (250 g) ground pork
2 beaten eggs
1 chopped onion
1 teaspoon salt
1 tablespoon chopped parsley
1 tablespoon chopped
  celery leaves
¼ cup Worcestershire sauce

2 tablespoons prepared
  horseradish
¼ cup of chopped green
  pepper
1 teaspoon dry mustard
1 ripe mashed banana
2 cups soft breadcrumbs
pinch herbs
Bacon strips

1. Mix all ingredients well and shape into a loaf.
2. Wrap strips of bacon around the meat loaf so that it is completely covered and fix them together with toothpicks.
3. Barbecue for about 1½ hours turning regularly or until it is done. (This can be tested by putting a skewer into the middle to see whether any blood is still running out.)

The loaf may also be barbecued in aluminum foil, but remove the foil during the last ½ hour of barbecuing.

Serves 4-6.

Skewered Beef Sesame

1 lb (500 g) Beef, round
  thickly cut
2 teaspoons lemon juice
1 tablespoon oil
1 tablespoon grated onion
¼ cup soya sauce

1 tablespoon brown sugar
1 tablespoon honey
2 cloves garlic, crushed
½ teaspoon ground ginger
1 tablespoon sesame seeds

1. Cut meat into 1 inch (2 cm) cubes.
2. Mix all the ingredients together and pour over beef.
3. Stir well and allow to sit for at least 2 hours at room temperature, turning over once or twice.
4. Thread meat onto skewers.
5. Cook over barbecue turning and basting with the remaining marinade for about 12 minutes. Roll in some additional sesame seeds and serve.

Serves 4.

Fillet Mignon

4 slices fillet steak
    cut 1½ inches (4 cm) thick
4 slices bacon
freshly ground black pepper
2 tablespoons (40 g) butter
2 tablespoons liverwurst
parsley
salt

1. Wrap a bacon slice around each slice of steak fastening with a toothpick.
2. Leave at room temperature for at least 20 minutes.
3. Sprinkle each side with ground black pepper and place a little butter on each steak.
4. Cook for 8 minutes each side spreading remaining butter when turning.
5. Season lightly with salt and spread liverwurst on top of each steak and return to barbecue for about 2 minutes.

Serves 4.

This steak is nice served with Barbecued Mushrooms (see recipe).

Fillet Steak

fillet of beef or tenderloin
peanut oil, salad oil
   or **olive oil**
garlic salt
pepper and salt
scallion
butter
salt
pepper

1. Marinate steak for 2-3 hours in oil. Use enough oil to cover side of steak. Liberally shake garlic salt over each side of steak. Turn 3 or 4 times.
2. Barbecue 8 minutes each side or until done to taste. Season.
3. Mince a scallion finely and mix into butter, add salt and pepper. Serve butter in balls on hot steak.

London Grill

one flank steak
2 tablespoons lemon juice
¼ cup oil
freshly ground black pepper
salt

1. Score the steak on each side in a criss-cross pattern.
2. Lay in a flat dish and pour on lemon juice and oil. Add pepper and allow to stand for 4 hours turning occasionally (place in refrigerator in hot weather)
3. Barbecue for 12 minutes on each side brushing occasionally with oil and lemon during cooking.
4. Lift onto a warm platter and season with salt. Allow to stand in a warm place for 5 minutes.
5. Carve downwards across the grain with a knife, at an angle of 45°. This method gives juicy slices of grilled steak as tender as many of the more expensive cuts.

Serves 4.

Carpetbag Steak

2 lb (1 kg) rump steak
cut 1½ inches (4 cm) thick
freshly ground black pepper
2 dozen oysters
juice of 1 lemon
nutmeg
1 tablespoon (20 g) butter
salt
1 teaspoon cornstarch

1. Leave steak at room temperature for 20 minutes.
2. Make a deep pocket in the steak.
3. Drain the oysters reserving liquor and some oysters.
4. Flavor oysters with lemon juice, nutmeg, salt and pepper. Put oysters in the pocket in the steak and close up and secure with toothpicks.
5. Barbecue turning and basting with half the butter for about 8 minutes each side or until done.
6. Meanwhile reduce oyster liquor in a saucepan to ½ cup (125 ml). Add reserved oysters, lemon juice salt and pepper to taste.
7. Mix cornstarch with a little cold water and thicken sauce. Cook for 1 minute. (This sauce can be made beforehand and heated just prior to serving).

Serves 4.

To serve, cut the steak into 1 inch (2 cm) thick slices with knife held at an angle to cut across the grain of the meat.

Curry Burgers

1 lb (500 g) ground beef
¼ cup dry breadcrumbs
1 egg
3 tablespoons cold water
2 tablespoons grated onion
1 teaspoon pepper
2 tablespoons chopped raisins
1 teaspoon curry powder

1. Mix all ingredients well together.
2. Shape into cakes and rub over each with a little oil.
3. Barbecue turning regularly.

Beef a La Lindstrom (Hamburgers)

1½ lb (750 g) ground round
8 oz (250 g) potatoes,
   cooked and mashed
1 large canned beet, grated
   or 1 large raw beet, grated
   and soaked in 2 tablespoons
   vinegar for 20 minutes
1 small onion, grated

2 tablespoons chopped capers
2 egg yolks
2 tablespoons thick cream
   (optional)
1½ teaspoons salt
freshly ground black pepper
butter or margarine for basting

1. Mix together beef, cold mashed potatoes, grated beet (drain off vinegar if raw beet is used), onion, capers, cream, salt and pepper.
2. Shape into flat cakes about 3 inches (8 cm) in diameter.
3. Cook over barbecue until brown and thoroughly cooked through.

Cheese and Bacon Burgers

1½ lb (750 g) ground round
1 cup blue vein cheese, crumbled
1 egg, beaten
grated rind of 1 lemon
1 teaspoon salt
3 tablespoons lemon juice
½ teaspoon freshly ground
   black pepper
6 slices bacon

1. Combine meat, cheese, egg, lemon rind, salt, lemon juice and black pepper.
2. Shape into cakes and wrap bacon around each securing with a toothpick.
3. Cook over barbecue turning regularly until done.

Serves 6.

These may be served with a slice of cheese or pineapple on top.

Tabasco Hamburgers

3 lb (1.5 kg) ground round
1 cup chopped onion
1 cup chopped green pepper
2 cups Hot Barbecue Sauce
   (see recipe)

1. Combine ground round, onion and green peppers with ¾ cup Hot Barbecue Sauce.
2. Shape into 12 hamburgers.
3. Barbecue basting frequently with Hot Barbecue Sauce.
4. Serve with remaining barbecue sauce.

Serves 6.

Hamcheezers

4 **tomatoes**
8 **split hamburger buns**
6 **oz (185 g) sliced ham**
½ **lb (250 g) shredded Swiss cheese**

Sauce:
½ **cup (125 g) butter**
   or **table margarine**
1 **tablespoon chopped green onions or chives**
1 **tablespoon chopped parsley**
1 **teaspoon dry mustard**
1 **clove garlic, chopped**

1. Mix all sauce ingredients together and spread onto buns.
2. Toss ham and cheese together and divide between 8 buns.
3. Press halves of buns together and then cut each into quarters. Thread onto skewers with quarters of tomatoes in between.
4. Wrap each in double thickness of aluminum foil sealing tightly.
5. Grill over hot fire for about 20 minutes or until done.

Lamb Chops

    6 lamb chops
    2 cloves garlic, crushed
    3 tablespoons olive oil
    2 teaspoons chopped parsley

1. Combine the garlic, olive oil and chopped parsley.
2. Split the chops and add a spoonful of the mixture to each pocket.
3. Cook over the barbecue until done brushing with additional garlic.

Buttermilk Lamb Kebabs

1½ lb (750 g) leg lamb, cut into 1 inch (2½ cm) cubes	12 large mushroom caps
1 cup (250 ml) buttermilk *or* skim milk yoghurt	2 zucchinis, sliced
½ teaspoon freshly ground black pepper	2 tablespoons oil
pinch of rosemary	2 green peppers, seeded and sliced
	8 tomatoes, quartered
	8 small onions

1. Mix buttermilk, pepper and rosemary together and pour over cubed lamb and marinate for at least 1 hour, turning occasionally.
2. Marinate the mushroom caps and zucchini slices in oil with a pinch of salt turning frequently.
3. Drain meat and arrange on skewers alternately with vegetables.
4. Cook over barbecue until meat is tender.

Serves 4.

Lamb and Eggplant Kebabs

2 lb (1 kg) lamb cut into
2 inch (5 cm) cubes
1 eggplant, cut into
2 inch (5 cm) cubes
12 small boiled potatoes
3 green peppers, each cut
into 6 sections

12 small whole onions
12 mushroom tops
2 cups of Hot Chilli Sauce
(see recipe)

1. Marinate lamb overnight in the Hot Chilli Sauce (see recipe).
2. Thread lamb with vegetables alternately onto skewers.
3. Cook over barbecue for 20 minutes basting with marinade.

Serves 6.

Lamb Kidney and Liver Kebabs

1 lb (500 g) lamb kidney
cut into 1 inch (2½ cm) cubes
1 lb (500 g) liver cut into
1 inch (2½ cm) cubes
1 lb (500 g) lamb cut into
1 inch (2½ cm) cubes

6 tomatoes, cut into cubes
12 mushrooms, tops only
2 onions, sliced
1 cup (250 g) melted butter
2 garlic cloves, crushed

1. Thread kidney, liver and lamb onto skewers alternating with tomato, mushrooms and onion slices.
2. Cook over barbecue 15 minutes, turning occasionally basting with butter and garlic mixed.

Serves 6.

Lamb Shanks Creole

½ cup tomato relish
   or tomato sauce
2 dessertspoons vinegar
½ cup (125 ml) dry red wine
2 dessertspoons oil
1 can (325 ml) condensed beef
   consomme
1 dessertspoon sugar
1 teaspoon salt
1 bay leaf
1 onion, chopped
6-8 lamb shanks

1. Mix all ingredients, except lamb shanks.
2. Place lamb shanks in the mixture and leave to stand at room temperature for at least 6 hours.
3. Place shanks in heavy duty foil. Turn foil up around the meat and pour in the remaining marinade. Close foil securely.
4. Place on barbecue and cook for 1 hour, turning once after half an hour.
5. Remove shanks from foil and place directly on the grill and cook for 4 minutes longer or until browned.

Devilled Lamb and Kidney en Brochette

1 breast lamb, boned
4 lamb kidneys
3 tablespoons (60 g) melted butter
½ teaspoon salt
freshly ground black pepper
1 tablespoon lemon juice
1 tablespoon Worcestershire sauce

1. Cut breast of lamb into 1½ inch (2 cm) squares.
2. Skin, cut into halves and core the kidneys.
3. Thread three pieces of lamb and 2 kidney pieces onto skewers, place on a dish.
4. Mix remaining ingredients together and brush over lamb and kidneys. Reserve any remaining devilled sauce.
5. Cook over barbecue for 15 minutes turning and basting occasionally with devilled sauce.

Serves 4.

Lamb Shanks with Vermouth

6 lamb shanks
1 cup (250 ml) dry vermouth
1 cup oil
2 tablespoons lemon juice
1 medium onion, chopped

1 garlic clove, crushed
1 teaspoon tarragon
1 teaspoon basil
1 teaspoon salt
freshly ground black pepper

1. Combine the oil, vermouth, lemon juice, garlic, herbs, salt and pepper.
2. Marinate the lamb shanks for at least 4 hours at room temperature turning and basting occasionally.
3. Cook lamb over barbecue for about 30 minutes basting frequently and turning.

This marinade can be used for lamb, chicken or pork.

Leg of Lamb

1 **leg of lamb, boned
and flattened**
1 **cup oil**
¼ **cup vinegar**
2 **garlic cloves, crushed**
1 **tablespoon salt**
freshly ground black pepper
Hot Barbecue Sauce (see recipe)

1. Combine oil, vinegar, garlic, salt and pepper.
2. Marinate lamb in the mixture at room temperature for at least 2 hours.
3. Baste and turn lamb occasionally while marinating.
4. Cook for 1½ to 2 hours turning frequently and basting with Hot Barbecue Sauce.

Serves 6.

Lamb Chops Italian Style

6 lamb chops
1 clove garlic, crushed
1 tablespoon grated
Parmesan cheese
¼ cup tomato sauce
1 tablespoon chopped parsley
⅛ teaspoon dried basil
freshly ground black pepper

1. Secure the tails of chops with a toothpick.
2. Mix tomato sauce, garlic, oil, cheese, parsley, basil, salt and pepper.
3. Place chops over barbecue and cook for 7 minutes or until done each side, basting several times with sauce.
4. Serve with the remaining warmed sauce.

Serves 6.

Rack of Lamb

3 loins of lamb
2 cloves garlic, crushed
3 tablespoons olive oil
2 teaspoons rosemary
salt
freshly ground black pepper

1. Rub crushed garlic and salt and pepper over all sides of loin of lamb.
2. Pour over the oil and sprinkle with rosemary.
3. Cook over barbecue for 1 hour or until done, basting occasionally with oil.

Serves 6-8.

Skewered Lamb Greek Style

2 lb (1 kg) boneless lamb,
   from leg preferably
small tomatoes or larger ones
   cut into quarters
zucchinis
small whole onions, par boiled
1 red and 1 green pepper
small mushrooms, tops only

Marinade:
¼ cup oil
½ cup lemon juice
½ cup white wine
1 teaspoon salt
freshly ground black
   pepper
½ teaspoon marjoram
2 cloves garlic, crushed
2 bay leaves, broken in pieces
1 tablespoon chopped mint

1. Cut meat in 1 inch (2½ cm) cubes.
2. Prepare the vegetables by cutting into 1 inch (2½ cm) cubes.
3. Mix all the ingredients of the marinade together in a bowl.
4. Mix in meat, cover and refrigerate for at least 8 hours turning occasionally.
5. Thread lamb onto skewers adding a piece of bay leaf between each piece of lamb.
6. Thread the vegetables, alternating them all, onto skewers.
7. Put lamb skewers onto barbecue and cook turning and brushing with the marinade during cooking.
8. Place the vegetable skewers on the barbecue after 10 minutes and brush and turn with marinade as well.

Serves 6.

This is nice served on plain boiled rice accompanied with tossed green salad and hot fresh bread.

Teriyaki Kebab

3 lb (1½ kg) lamb, cut
   into 2 inch (5 cm) cubes
1 cup (250 ml) pineapple juice
2 tablespoons soya sauce
2 tablespoons lemon juice
2 garlic cloves, crushed
2 cups canned pineapple chunks

1. Combine pineapple juice, soya sauce, lemon juice and garlic.
2. Marinate the lamb cubes in the mixture for at least 2 hours at room temperature.
3. Thread lamb and pineapple chunks alternately onto the skewers.
4. Cook over barbecue for 10 minutes, basting frequently with the marinade.

Serves 6.

Ham Steaks

6 ham steaks
3 cups sherry
½ cup (125 g) butter, melted
3 tablespoons dry mustard
½ cup brown sugar
2 cloves garlic, crushed
paprika

1. Mix sherry, butter, mustard, brown sugar, garlic and paprika.
2. Marinate ham steaks in the mixture for at least 2 hours.
3. Baste and turn ham steaks in marinade occasionally.
4. Cook over barbecue turning and basting frequently with marinade.

Serves 6.

Russian Shaslik

1½ lb (750 g) boned and trimmed
   lamb, leg shoulder *or* loin
8 oz (250 g) bacon slices
6 small tomatoes

Marinade:
½ cup (125 ml) vodka
4 tablespoons oil
juice of 1 lemon
1 bay leaf
pinch of thyme, rosemary,
   dill, cumin, salt
freshly ground black
   pepper

1. Cut meat into 1 inch (2 cm) cubes.
2. Mix all the marinade ingredients together in a large bowl.
3. Put meat into marinade and let stand at room temperature for at least 8 hours (place in refrigerator in hot weather). Then move to refrigerator for 40 hours.
4. Cut each slice in three and roll up.
5. When ready to barbecue place meat and bacon rolls alternately on skewers finishing with a tomato.
6. Cook on barbecue for 8-12 minutes, basting occasionally with oil from marinade.

Serves 6.

Minted Lamb Chops

4-6   loin lamb chops,
   cut thickly
2 tablespoons lemon juice
2 tablespoons oil
2 tablespoons mint jelly
1 tablespoon freshly chopped mint

1. Secure the tails of the chops with toothpicks.
2. Place on a plate and rub lemon juice into each side of chops, then rub in the oil.
3. Allow to stand for at least 1 hour.
4. Place the chops on the barbecue and cook for 2 minutes each side.
5. Brush the top with some mint jelly and cook for 3 minutes. Turn and brush the remaining mint jelly. Cook until done.
6. Serve with chopped mint sprinkled over each top.

Serves 4-6.

Serve with minted potatoes, glazed carrots and green vegetables.

Honey-Fruit Pork Chops

6 pork chops
1 cup pineapple
   or **orange juice**
1 teaspoon curry powder
¼ cup honey
1 clove garlic, crushed
freshly ground black pepper
¼ cup salad oil

1. Mix all ingredients together.
2. Marinate pork chops in the mixture at room temperature for 1 hour.
3. Cook over barbecue for 25 minutes each side or until done.

Serves 6.

This marinade may be used for lamb and chicken.

Ham with Pineapple

6 slices of lean ham
4 tablespoons (80 g) butter
6 rings canned pineapple
watercress to garnish

Sauce:
2 onions, grated
4 tablespoons (80 g) butter
3 tablespoons flour
3 cups (750 ml) milk
salt
freshly ground pepper
8 tablespoons cooked corn
6 tablespoons parsley
4 tablespoons syrup from can
**   of pineapple**

1. Baste ham with melted butter.
2. Cook over barbecue until ham is nearly done.
3. Baste pineapple with melted butter and cook over barbecue.
4. Meanwhile chop onion.
5. Melt butter in pan and stir in the flour and cook for two minutes.
6. Gradually add milk and then onions and cook until thickened, stirring all the time.
7. Add corn, salt, pepper and parsley and keep warm.
8. Just before serving the ham steaks add the pineapple syrup.

Serves 6.

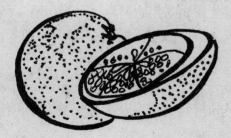

Marinated Pork Fillets

1 lb (500 g) pork tenderloin
2 tablespoons soya sauce
1 teaspoon brandy
1 teaspoon sugar
2 teaspoons salt
clove of garlic,
    finely chopped
1 small piece of green
    ginger (optional)

1. Mix all ingredients together.
2. Allow pork tenderloin to marinate for at least 1 hour at room temperature.
3. Barbecue slowly turning frequently and basting with the remaining marinade.

Pork Chops

6 pork chops
1 cup soya sauce
1 garlic clove, crushed
freshly ground black pepper
1 cup (250 ml) Hot Chili Sauce
    (see recipes)

1. Combine soya sauce, garlic and pepper.
2. Marinate chops in the mixture for at least 1 hour turning and basting frequently with marinade.
3. Cook at least 30 minutes on each side basting frequently with Hot Chili Sauce.

Serves 6.

Oriental Barbecued Pork Chops

6 rib pork chops
grated rind of 1 orange
juice of 1 orange
4 tablespoons (80 g) butter
salt
freshly ground black pepper
1 teaspoon ginger, ground
4 teaspoons flour
2 tablespoons dry sherry
2 teaspoons brown sugar

1. Rub orange rind into meat surface and sprinkle with ginger and allow to stand for 10 minutes.
2. Barbecue the chops for 14 minutes each side basting with a mixture of orange juice and 2 tablespoons butter.
3. Meanwhile make the sauce by putting 2 tablespoons of butter into a saucepan and stir in flour and cook 1 minute.
4. Remove from heat and stir in orange juice, sherry and sugar.
5. Return to heat and continue stirring until sauce thickens. (This sauce may be made beforehand and heated just prior to serving.)

Serves 6.

These chops can be made to look attractive if you garnish them with warmed slices of orange.

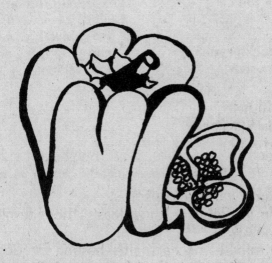

Spare Ribs

5 lb (2½ kg) spare ribs
(pork or beef)
½ cup (125 ml) Cointreau
½ cup soya sauce
½ cup honey
1 cup canned crushed
pineapple

½ cup vinegar
1 lemon, sliced
2 teaspoons ground ginger
¼ cup brown sugar
2 cloves garlic, crushed
1 teaspoon dry mustard
fresh ground black pepper

1. Combine Cointreau, soya sauce, honey, pineapple, vinegar, lemon slices, ginger, brown sugar, garlic, mustard and pepper.
2. Marinate spare ribs in the mixture for at least 1 hour at room temperature.
3. Remove lemon slices.
4. Cook spare ribs over barbecue for 20 minutes each side basting frequently with marinade.

Serves 6.

Pork Satay

1 lb (500 g) pork fillet
or leg
½ teaspoon salt
freshly ground black pepper
2 tablespoons almonds,
ground
1 small piece root ginger, grated
or ½ teaspoon ground ginger

1 teaspoon turmeric
1 clove garlic, crushed
2 teaspoons brown sugar
1 cup (250 ml) Coconut Milk
(see recipe)

1. Cut pork into 1 inch (2 cm) cubes. Season with salt and pepper.
2. Mix ground almonds, ginger, turmeric, garlic, sugar in basin.
3. Blend in Coconut Milk and add pork.
4. Stir well and allow to marinate for at least 3 hours at room temperature.
5. Remove pork and thread onto skewers.
6. Cook over barbecue, turning and basting with the spiced Coconut Milk. The remaining Coconut Milk may be heated and served with the satay.

Serves 4.

Chicken Livers

3 chicken livers	1 tablespoon (20 g) butter
6 slices bacon	per serving
1 lb (500 g) mushrooms	salt
parsley	freshly ground black pepper
chives snipped	

1. Cut livers in half, wrap each in a slice of bacon.
2. Thread onto skewers and grill for 7 minutes over barbecue.
3. Wrap mushrooms in 6 foil packages with parsley, chives, salt and freshly ground pepper.
4. Cook over fire for 10 minutes each side.
5. Open packages and serve with sprinkled parsley and chives.

Serves 6.

Chicken Wings

1 lb (500 g) chicken wings	1 teaspoon honey
3 tablespoons soya sauce	1 tablespoon catsup
3 tablespoons lemon juice	salt
⅛ teaspoon onion powder	white pepper
or ½ teaspoon grated onion	

1. Using kitchen shears, cut off outer wing tips. Divide each wing into 2 parts at the joint and put in a bowl.
2. Mix soya sauce, lemon juice and onion and pour over chicken.
3. Cover loosely and marinate in refrigerator several hours or overnight.
4. Mix honey and tomato sauce with 1 tablespoon marinade and brush half in wings. Sprinkle with salt and pepper and cook over barbecue for about 15 minutes, turn and brush with remaining baste and cook a further 15 minutes.

Serves 4.

Chicken in Wine

3 2 lb (1 kg) chickens cut up
1 cup (250 ml) white wine
½ cup oil
1 teaspoon chopped chives
1 tablespoon chopped parsley
1 teaspoon basil

1. Combine, wine, oil, chives, parsley and basil and marinate chicken pieces for at least 1 hour at room temperature.
2. Cook over barbecue for at least 30 minutes or until done turning frequently and basting with marinade.

Serves 6.

Chicken Pieces

chicken pieces (allow ¾ lb
(375 g) per person)
1 lemon
½ cup (125 g) melted butter
salt
freshly ground black pepper
paprika

1. Rub the chicken pieces with a mixture of the lemon, melted butter, salt, pepper and paprika.
2. Cook over barbecue until golden brown.

Chicken on a Spit with Brazil Nuts

3 2 lb (1 kg) chickens with livers
1 cup of chopped brazil nuts
1 cup (250 g) butter
½ cup chopped onions
1 cup chopped celery
   with leaves
8 oz (250 g) stuffing mix
½ teaspoon thyme
½ teaspoon basil
1 cup (250 ml) chicken stock
salt
freshly ground black pepper

1. Sauté chicken livers in ½ cup (125 g) butter until lightly browned.
2. Cut up the livers.
3. Sauté brazil nuts, onion and celery in butter left in the pan for 10 minutes.
4. Mix the nuts with stuffing mix.
5. Add thyme, basil and chicken stock, together with livers, toss lightly together.
6. Rub chicken inside and outside with salt and pepper and fill loosely with stuffing.
7. Melt the remaining ½ cup (125 g) butter.
8. Place chickens on spit over barbecue, brush with butter and cook basting for 1½ hours or until done.

Serves 4 to 6.

Oriental Chicken

4 chicken halves
1 cup soya sauce
1 cup (250 ml) sherry
1 teaspoon ginger
1 teaspoon mustard
sesame seeds

1. Combine soya sauce, sherry, ginger and mustard.
2. Marinate the chicken in the mixture at room temperature for at least 1 hour.
3. Barbecue until crisp and golden brown, basting frequently with the remaining marinade.
4. When chicken pieces are ready, press the skin into the sesame seeds.
5. Return to barbecue for 2 minutes or until the seeds are toasted.

Serves 4.

Duck on a Spit

2 ducks
½ cup brandy
4 oranges
½ cup oil
1 cup (250 g) butter
1 cup (250 ml) orange juice
grated rind of 2 oranges

1. Soak 2 peeled oranges in brandy.
2. Stuff the ducks with the marinated oranges.
3. Brush the ducks with the oil and barbecue for 1½ hours or until done.
4. Meanwhile combine butter, orange juice and rind and simmer for 15 minutes stirring occasionally.
5. Serve the ducks with the orange butter sauce.

Serves 6.

Cumberland Chicken

3   2 lb (1 kg) chicken cut
into pieces
4   tablespoons (80 g) butter
melted
3   tablespoons of lime juice
(sweetened)
1   cup red currant jam
1   can concentrated orange juice
(frozen)
5   tablespoons dry sherry
1   teaspoon dry mustard
¼   teaspoon ginger
¼   teaspoon Tabasco sauce
1   teaspoon salt
freshly ground black pepper

1. Season chicken with salt and pepper.
2. Combine melted butter and lime juice and baste chicken with the mixture.
3. Cook over a barbecue for 35 to 50 minutes turning and basting with mixture.
4. Meanwhile combine red currant jam, orange juice, sherry, mustard, ginger, Tabasco sauce and a pinch of salt and pepper.
5. Simmer over low heat until smooth and hot.
6. Serve sauce with the chicken.

Serves 6.

Milano Chicken

6 pieces of chicken	9 large ripe olives
3 teaspoons oil	6 tablespoons tomato sauce
1 teaspoon salt	1 teaspoon basil
2 medium potatoes, pared	3 tablespoons (60 g) butter
salt	*or* margarine
3 medium zucchini	

1. Brush chicken pieces with oil and sprinkle with salt.
2. Cut potatoes lengthwise into slices.
3. Place potatoes on a large piece of double thickness aluminum foil and sprinkle with salt.
4. Cut unpared zucchini into rounds and place on potatoes and sprinkle with salt.
5. Top with chicken pieces, olives, tomato sauce and basil. Dot with butter and wrap up securely.
6. Cook for 30 minutes on each side or until chicken and vegetables are tender.
7. Open packet and sprinkle with Parmesan cheese before serving.

Serves 6.

Orange Duck

    5 lb (2½ kg) duck
    1 teaspoon salt
    1 clove garlic, crushed
    2 whole black peppers
    2 unpeeled oranges, quartered
    ½ cup orange marmalade
       or apricot preserve

1. Wash duck under cold water. Drain and dry.
2. Fasten skin of neck of duck over back.
3. Salt inside and place garlic, pepper and orange pieces in the cavity.
4. Secure with poultry pins, lace with twine.
5. Insert spit through center of duck.
6. Cook over barbecue for at least 2 hours pricking the skin with a skewer from time to time to release fat to drain away.
7. Spread orange marmalade all over duck approximately 10 minutes before bird is ready to serve.

Serves 4.

Devilled Cheese Stuffed Frankfurters

    1 cup shredded processed cheese
    ⅓ cup pickle relish
    1 teaspoon prepared mustard
    1 tablespoon chilli sauce
    3 tablespoons salad dressing
       or mayonnaise
    1 lb (500 g) frankfurters

1. Have cheese at room temperature and mix with a fork until smooth and soft.
2. Add remaining ingredients except frankfurters, and mix well.
3. Split frankfurters lengthwise almost all the way through. Fill with cheese mixture.
4. Grill over barbecue until heated and cheese mixture is slightly melted.

Serves 4.

Pigs in Blankets

1 lb (500 g) cocktail frankfurters
½ lb (250 g) bacon slices
barbecue or tomato sauce
   (Apricot Barbecue Sauce see recipe)

1. Cut bacon into 3 inch (5 cm) strips. Lay 1 frankfurter on each strip and brush with sauce.
2. Roll up and barbecue for 3 minutes or until bacon is crispy brown.
3. Serve on a platter and use sauce in a bowl as a dip.

Serves 4.

Frankfurter Kebabs

frankfurters and rolls
pineapple chunks
salad oil

1. Cut frankfurters into 5 pieces.
2. Alternating frankfurter pieces and pineapple, thread the pieces onto a skewer.
3. Brush over with oil.
4. Barbecue over fire from 7 to 10 minutes, turning frequently.
5. During the last few minutes toast the rolls, which have already been buttered, cut side down on the grill.
6. Serve kebabs on the rolls with mustard or barbecue sauce.

Sausages Française

    6 french rolls
    6 large sausages already
       barbecued
    garlic butter
    chopped chives
    parsley
    6 slices cheese

1. Mix garlic butter, chopped chives and parsley, and butter the rolls.
2. Place the barbecued sausages on the buttered rolls.
3. Add a slice of cheese to the rolls and wrap tightly in a piece of aluminum foil.
4. Cook over the barbecue until the cheese melts.

Serves 6.

Sausage Sizzlers

    ¼ lb (250 g) ground pork and
       ¼ lb ground beef
    2 teaspoons Worcestershire sauce
    1 level tablespoon tomato
       chutney
    dash Tabasco sauce
    8 slices bread from a large white,
       ready sliced loaf
    tomato slices
    thinly sliced onion rings
    parsley sprigs

1. Blend together the meats, Worcestershire sauce, chutney and Tabasco sauce.
2. Toast one side of each slice of bread over coals, spread some of the sausage meat right up to the edge of the untoasted side of bread.
3. Cook uncooked side for about 7 minutes or until sausage meat is done.
4. Slice in half and serve with tomato, onion ring and parsley.

Serves 4.

Sausages with Liverwurst

6 knockwurst sausages
½ lb (250 g) liverwurst
2 tablespoons grated onion
½ cup sour cream
Tabasco sauce

1. Mash the liverwurst and combine with the grated onion and sour cream and a dash of Tabasco sauce.
2. Slice along the top of the sausages and stuff the sausages with the mixture.
3. Brush the sausages with mustard and roll each two in aluminum foil.
4. Cook over barbecue for 15 minutes turning them twice, uncover and crisp the sausages for a minute or two over the fire.

Serves 6.

Bologna Roll (On Spit)

1 3 lb (1½ kg) bologna roll
2 tablespoons prepared mustard
1 cup orange marmalade
cooked whole potatoes

1. Remove casing from sausage. Score a criss cross pattern on the sausage, center on spit making sure it is well centered in place by skewers.
2. Cook, brushing occasionally with mixture of mustard and marmalade, 1 to 1½ hours depending on the thickness and temperature. Shortly before serving, brush potatoes with butter and put on rack over heat.

Serves 6.

Hot Dogs

12 frankfurters
Hot Chilli Sauce (see recipe)

1. Barbecue the frankfurters for 10 minutes turning frequently.
2. Serve with Hot Chilli Sauce on bread rolls.

Serves 6.

Carpetbag Sausages

12 large German Sausages
2 bottles oysters

1. Barbecue sausages slowly, turning frequently.
2. Slice along the length of the sausages and fill with oysters.

Serves 6.

Fish with Spinach Stuffing

4 **lb to 5 lb (1 kg to 1½ kg) whole**
  snapper or trout
4 **tablespoons (80 g) melted**
  butter
1¼ **cups (300 ml) dry white wine**
½ **oz (15 g) soft butter**
parsley
slices of lemon

Stuffing:
3 **tablespoons (60 g) butter**
2 **tablespoons chopped scallions**
  or **spring onions**
½ **lb (15 g) chopped cooked**
  fresh spinach squeezed dry and
  packed down firmly
  or **10 oz (315 g) package frozen**
  chopped spinach, defrosted and
  squeezed dry
2½ **cups fresh white breadcrumbs**
2 **tablespoons thick cream**
lemon juice
½ **teaspoon salt**
freshly ground black pepper

1. Make the stuffing by melting the butter over a moderate heat.
2. Add the scallions, cook for about 2 minutes, do not brown.
3. Add the spinach and cook over high heat, stirring constantly, for 3 minutes to evaporate any moisture.
4. Put the mixture into a large bowl and add crumbs, cream, lemon juice to taste, salt and pepper and toss gently together.
5. Stuff the fish with the mixture and close the opening. Brush the fish with a mixture of 3 tablespoons butter, salt, pepper and wine.
6. Place the fish on double aluminum foil and pour over the butter and wine. Close tightly.
7. Cook over the barbecue for about 10 minutes each side or until done.

Serves 4.

Fish

fish (one small whole fish
  per person or 1 large fish)
butter
lemon
onion
parsley
salt
freshly ground black pepper

1. Place fish on buttered foil.
2. Stuff each fish with a slice of lemon, onion and a sprig of parsley and sprinkle the cavity with salt and freshly ground pepper.
3. Rub butter all over the skin of the fish and tightly seal the aluminum foil.
4. Bake over coals of fire for approximately 10 minutes each side or until done.

Shrimp and Bacon Kebab

3 lb (1½ kg) shelled shrimp
1 lb (500 g) sliced bacon
1 cup soya sauce
½ cup lemon juice
2 cups canned pineapple chunks,
  drained
sprig of mint

1. Mix soya sauce and lemon juice together.
2. Marinate the shrimp in marinade for at least 30 minutes.
3. Thread shrimp, pineapple chunks, mint and folded bacon alternately onto skewers.
4. Cook over barbecue until bacon is crisp.

Serves 4-6.

Shrimp

2 lb (1 kg) raw or cooked shrimp
2 garlic cloves, crushed
½ teaspoon black pepper
½ cup (125 g) butter
    or **margarine**
½ teaspoon salt
½ cup chopped parsley
juice of 1 lemon

1. Peel and de-vein shrimp.
2. Blend butter with remaining ingredients.
3. Tear off 6, 9 inch (23 cm) strips of heavy duty aluminum foil and fold each in half to make a 9 inch (23 cm) square.
4. Divide the shrimp equally on pieces of foil.
5. Top each with 1/6th of butter mixture.
6. Bring foil up around shrimp and seal tightly.
7. Barbecue 5 to 10 minutes.

Serves 6.

Oyster Kebab

2 doz oysters
    (fresh or bottled)
24 strips bacon
lemon juice
freshly ground black pepper

1. Drain oysters.
2. Season with lemon and pepper.
3. Wrap each oyster in a strip of bacon and thread onto a skewer, leave a small space between each wrapped oyster.
4. Cook over a barbecue for 15 minutes or until the bacon becomes crisp.

Serves 4.

Lobster

1 lb to 1½ lb (500 g to 750 g)
  lobster per person
½ cup (125 g) butter
2 tablespoons parsley
juice of 1 lemon

1. Split the lobster lengthwise and clean if the lobster has not already been done so by the fish dealer.
2. Spread the lobster open as far as possible. Lift out and discard the dark vein down the center and the small sac about 3 inches (6 cm) long just below the head.
3. Place the lobster on the grill shellside down. Barbecue 15 minutes.
4. Brush lobster generously with the melted butter, parsley and lemon juice mixed together.
5. Sprinkle with salt and pepper and barbecue another 5 minutes or until done.
6. Serve with the remaining melted butter, parsley and lemon juice.

Fish with Caper Sauce

fish steaks
2 tablespoons (40 g) butter,
  melted
1 tablespoon lemon juice
freshly ground black pepper

Sauce:
½ cup (125 g) butter
½ cup capers
grated rind of 1 lemon
juice of 1 lemon
¼ cup sweet pickles, chopped

1. Cut the fish into 1 inch (3 cm) pieces.
2. Marinate the fish in the butter and lemon juice mixed together for 5 minutes.
3. Barbecue over a fire for about 5 minutes. Brush with some more butter and lemon juice, turn and cook a further 5 minutes.
4. Meanwhile mix all the sauce ingredients together in a bowl that can be placed over the fire and leave until the sauce becomes thick and creamy. Do not overheat or the butter will become too liquid.

Serves 4-6.

Scallop Kebabs

1 lb (500 g) fresh or frozen
  scallops
1 can small mushrooms, drained
2 tablespoons salad oil
2 tablespoons soya sauce
2 tablespoons lemon juice

2 tablespoons chopped parsley
½ teaspoon salt
freshly ground black pepper
12 bacon slices
1 can pineapple chunks
sprinkle of nutmeg

1. Thaw scallops if frozen and wash and remove any shell particles.
2. Place scallops and mushrooms in shallow glass dish.
3. Combine oil, soya sauce, lemon juice, parsley, salt, pepper and nutmeg and pour over the scallops.
4. Let stand at room temperature for at least 1 hour.
5. Partially fry bacon, cut each slice in half.
6. Remove mushrooms and scallops from marinade and alternately thread them onto a skewer with bacon.
7. Cook over barbecue from 6 to 9 minutes on each side.

Serves 4.

Fish Sticks Barbecued

12 fish sticks
½ cup (125 g) melted butter
½ cup lemon juice
parsley
capers

Sauce:
½ cup tomato sauce
1 onion, grated
chopped chives
2 tablespoons lemon juice

1. Place frozen sticks on plate.
2. Combine the butter with the lemon juice and brush over the fish sticks.
3. Place over the hot barbecue and cook each side until they are brown on all sides.
4. Mix all the ingredients for the sauce together either while the fish sticks are cooking or you can prepare the sauce well in advance. The sauce may be served hot or cold over the fish. Sprinkle them with some capers and parsley.

Serves 4-6.

Oyster and Scallop Kebab

2 doz oysters, fresh
   or bottled
2 doz scallops
1 can sliced pineapple
butter, melted
freshly ground black pepper

1. Drain the oysters and the pineapple.
2. Melt some butter, add to the pineapple juice. Set aside.
3. Thread the oysters, scallops and pineapple slices alternately onto a skewer. Brush over with either the butter and pineapple juice or oil and pineapple juice.
4. Barbecue over hot coals until they are just browning, about 7 minutes. Baste with the remaining butter or oil and pineapple juice.

Serves 4-6.

Marinated Barbecue Shrimp

24 large green shrimp, shelled,
deveined and tails left on
24 slices bacon, rind removed
2 large onions, sliced

Marinade:
2 cloves garlic
2 tablespoons brown sugar
3 tablespoons soya sauce
3 tablespoons dry sherry
½ teaspoon ground ginger
½ teaspoon mace
½ teaspoon chilli powder

1. Cut the shrimp down one side and open out like a butterfly.
2. Place a slice of onion on the shrimp and roll up and wrap in a slice of bacon and hold together with a toothpick.
3. Mix all the ingredients together for the marinade and pour over the shrimp rolls and leave to marinate for at least 1 hour. Turn the shrimp two or three times.
4. Barbecue over a medium fire until the shrimp are cooked and the bacon crispy.

Serves 4-6.

Index

Lobster pie 90
Lobster souffle 87
Lobster stew 89
Lobster Thermidor 88
Lobster with tomato cream sauce 86
Lamb and eggplant kebabs 64
Lamb chops 63
Lamb chops Italian style 68
Lamb, kidney and liver kebabs 64
Lamb shanks creole 65
Lamb shanks with vermouth 66
Leg of lamb 67
Lime and honey salad dressing 19
Lobster 91
London Grill 58

Maitre d'hotel butter 15
Mango salad 51
Marinated barbecued shrimp 94
Marinated cucumber 39
Marinated mushrooms Greek style 50
Marinated pork fillets 74
Mayonnaise (blender version) 18
Milano chicken 82
Minted lamb chops 72
Mock pate 22
Mushroom salad 47
Mushrooms, baked 40

Onion, baked 39
Onion dip 22
Orange duck 83
Orange salad 52
Oriental chicken 80
Oriental barbecued pork chops 75
Oyster and scallop kebab 93
Oyster kebab 90

Peach kebab 54
Peanut butter sauce 10
Pigs in blankets 84
Pineapple and walnut dip 21
Plum soup, cold 28
Plum sauce 9
Pork chops 74
Pork Satay 76
Potatoes in foil, baked 38

Quick cream of spinach soup 27

Rack of lamb 68
Ratatouille 39
Russian shaslik 71

Salade Nicoise 41
Sausages with potato salad 44
Sausages Francaise 85
Sausage sizzlers 85
Sausages with liverwurst 86
Scallop kebabs 92
Shrimp and bacon kebab 89
Shrimp 90
Skewered beef sesame 56

Skewered lamb Greek style 69
Smoked oyster dip 21
Sour cream mayonnaise 17
Spare ribs 76
Spiced bananas 54
Spiced yoghurt dip 20
Steak sauce 11
Stuffed green peppers 36
Sweet cole slaw 40
Sweet corn 37

Teriyaki kebab 70
Tabasco hamburgers 61
Tomato and cucumber salad 46
Tomato aspic 35
Tomatoes 35
Tomato puff 34
Tomato salad dressing 17

Watercress soup 28
Western meat loaf 56
Wine vinegar dressing 19

Zucchinis 31
Zucchinis, boiled 31